THE
GOOD
LIFE
RULES

THE
GOOD LIFE RULES

8 KEYS TO BEING YOUR BEST AT WORK AND AT PLAY

BRYAN DODGE

WITH MATTHEW RUDY

McGraw Hill

New York Chicago San Francisco Lisbon London Madrid Mexico City
Milan New Delhi San Juan Seoul Singapore Sydney Toronto

10 11 12 13 14 15 16 17   QFR/QFR   1 9 8 7 6 5 4

ISBN 978-0-07-150838-4
MHID   0-07-150838-4

Library of Congress Cataloging-in-Publication Data

Dodge, Bryan.
    The good life rules : eight keys to being your best at work and play / by Bryan Dodge and Matt Rudy.
        p.   cm.
    ISBN 978-0-07-150838-4 (alk. paper)
    MHID   0-07-150838-4 (alk. paper)
    1. Success—Psychological aspects. I. Rudy, Matthew.   II. Title.

BF637.S8D57   2009
158—dc22   2008023018

McGraw-Hill books are available at special quantity discounts to use as premiums and sales promotions or for use in corporate training programs. To contact a representative, please e-mail us at bulksales@mcgraw-hill.com.

Contents

Acknowledgments.. vii

Introduction.. xi

Rule 1: The Fundamental Rule: Be Willing to Change........... 1

Rule 2: Be a Learner.. 21

Rule 3: Get to the Why in Life, or the EAT Plan................. 37

Rule 4: Diminishing Intent, or Follow Your Heart in
Forty-Eight Hours.. 53

Rule 5: Be Faithful.. 69

Rule 6: Create New Habits.. 87

Rule 7: Be a Leader.. 105

Rule 8: Find the Balance Between Work and Home........... 133

Bringing It All Together.. 149

Epilogue.. 163

Appendix.. 165

Recommended Reading.. 171

Index.. 181

Acknowledgments

All the internal and external battles and mountains I had to climb to finally get this message into a book—and into your hands—would have been in vain without the help of some exceptional people in my life. I'm truly humbled by all the support you all have given me. You gave me time to develop, and you never lost faith in my ability to deliver this message.

I wouldn't have been able to do what I love so much without the continuing support of more than 21,000 companies, organizations, trade associations, and community groups. You all have been generous enough to give me a chance to make a difference with your people—and you've kept giving me those chances year after year. I make more than 300 appearances a year, and a giant majority of those are repeat business to groups I've spoken to before, and referrals from people who know what I do. That's a great, great honor.

Your friendships and your willingness to support me and my family are what made this book possible. So I dedicate *The Good Life Rules* to all the people who have attended one of my programs over the last eighteen years, to the organizations that took a chance on me when I was a struggling unknown, and to the people who give up some time from their weekends to listen to my radio show on WBAP in Dallas.

The stories in this book are my life, but I wouldn't have been able to figure out a way to organize and tell them if I hadn't found Matt Rudy. He's a fantastic writer—even when the subject isn't golf—and he's a great friend. Our chemistry was better than I could have even hoped, and I'm glad I listened to my own advice about listening to advice from good people. He made this book sound more like me than I ever could have. I'm looking forward to working with him on many other projects.

Johanna Bowman at McGraw-Hill saw something great in our proposal, and she stuck with us when a lot of editors might have given up. Thanks for being so patient! And the book never would have gotten off the ground without Farley Chase and Terry Whalin.

My business partner, Frank Massine, has been the best partner and friend anybody could ever ask for, and I'm so grateful for all the support he and his family have given me. Without Bonnie Shumate keeping me in line at the office, I'd never know what city I was in or how to get home. She's made me look so much better than I deserve.

I want to thank my mom and dad, Dick and Betty Dodge, for always sticking with me. They are my best friends, and they've given me unconditional support, dedication, and true love. My brother, Dick, gave me a one-on-one talk that made the difference for life, and my sister, Kathleen, has always helped me stand strong.

Most of all, I want to reach deep into my heart and thank my wife, Margaret. She's been my best friend, my girlfriend, my partner—and my soul mate—for more than thirty years. Together, we have three of the greatest gifts you can have: my daughter, Nicole, brings faith and hope; my son Johnathan has taught me to never give up; and my son Zach truly has a great heart. Thanks to all of you for making a great team called "family."

A lot of the strength on our team has come thanks to Margaret's family, the Smiths. They accepted me into their warm—and huge—family and taught me so much about loyalty and trust from the inside out, and about truly enjoying life. Margaret's dad, Page, and her mom, Helen, were an inspiration, and it makes me smile when I think of how they used to say, "Man, this is living!"

I also want to acknowledge my Lord and Savior—the Giver of great gifts, who has given me the passion to encourage others not just to know Him, but to know and understand how important you really are and how you do matter in this world. And how you are called to make a difference.

The Good Life Rules!

Introduction

Last year I got up in front of more than three hundred groups and relayed the message you're about to read in this book: that anyone can learn and live by The Good Life Rules; that anyone can use these tools to get up tomorrow and let go of yesterday's mistakes and procrastinations to be happier and more satisfied with life.

And, most important, that anyone can learn how to bring energy and passion home for the most important people in life: the people who count on you every day. It's going to sound funny, but I didn't write this book for you. I wrote this book for the people depending on you: your family. The most important people in your life.

You picked up this book because you were looking for something, right? Or somebody gave you this book as a gift, because they thought you might find something in it that would help. Maybe you're the person who gives twelve hours of effort during a workday, and when you get home, you're just hoping for some quiet. The way it ends up, you have energy for the people whom you don't really know, and you're out of it for the people who have given you their life.

It's no wonder, then, that you're looking for the golden nugget that would somehow transform your hectic life into something more balanced. Something happier.

I've been fortunate to meet tens of thousands of people just like you. Heck, I was you. I was the guy who said yes to everything. I started a company that connected expert personal and educational speakers with corporate America. After some lean years, we really started doing well, and I had more than one hundred employees working for me. But one Sunday, I brought my young son with me to my office so I could get some work done, and he started building a chain of paper clips.

The next time I looked up, he had a strand of clips that went the entire length of our building. Standing there with the end of his chain, he asked me, "Dad, why did you start this company?"

I said, "So I could spend more time with you."

"So how come it isn't working?" he asked.

That just stopped me right in my tracks. I knew it was time to make a change.

Since then, I've reorganized my life. I used to be the guy behind the desk who tried to find the right speaker to deliver a message to my clients. But for the last eighteen years, I've been the one sharing the message myself, to tens of thousands of people as a personal development speaker.

I've been sharing the message that you can balance your work life and home life. You can develop yourself professionally, achieve all your goals, and still have energy for your family when you get home at night. You can have The Good Life. I'll show you how over the next nine chapters, but here's a hint about how I learned these lessons.

As I said, I spoke to more than three hundred groups last year—from Fortune 500 companies to local community organizations—in forty-two states and Canada. But I was in hotel rooms only forty-one nights.

Why?

Because I have a crush on Margaret, the girl I married thirty years ago. She was there in the beginning, when I was a jock with a bad attitude and a learning disability. I was the guy who had to keep a second set of clothes in the truck for when I sweated through the first set, because I was so nervous about what other people thought of me when I got up to speak in high school. When we were in college, Margaret taught me the value of learning and the value of self-confidence, and those are gifts I've appreciated every day of my life since then. My three kids, Nicole, Johnathan, and Zach, are my best buddies. And as much as I get a charge out of helping great folks like you around this country, I have even more fun with my family—whether we're going waterskiing at the lake near our house outside of Dallas or just hanging out with the horse and the Labs. If you want to know who I am, come meet my family when I'm not around. It's the true test, and I'm so proud of them.

From the time that I was a struggling pharmaceutical salesman in Sioux City, Iowa, I was never the guy who could float into the room without any preparation whatsoever and make the sale. I was never the smartest guy, or the one who had the most natural gifts. I have never taken the easy route, because I can't afford to. I'm persistent, I'm optimistic, and I have been blessed with a tremendous amount of energy; and I was taught to work hard.

Those things have set me up to make some tremendous mistakes, and I've made them. I can't thank my mom, dad, and all of my family enough for sticking with me. But I've always chosen to get back into the game of life, by choosing to get back up when I've been knocked down. Today, I have The Good Life. And better yet, I know it's something every single person can get—and maintain. In this book, I'm going to help you figure out what The Good Life is for you, how to recognize the good things in your life before you lose them, and the strategies for bringing your work and home lives into balance.

This isn't some kind of Hollywood promise—that you're going to be a millionaire overnight, lose thirty pounds by the end of the month, and become the most popular person in the break room at your office. One of my favorite stories to tell is about this fantasy couple that falls in love and marries. They're perfect communicators, they're perfect with money, and they're perfect in how they handle their relationship. This is perfectly hypothetical, of course. This perfect couple decides that they're going to keep everything exactly the same, but have children. Now, I believe that children are the greatest gift you can get, but there's a price you pay for them—and sleep and quiet are just the start. You have to be ready to change, because a two-week-old baby isn't going to change for you.

The Good Life Rules work the same way. Just like there's a price to pay for children, there's a price to pay for success. There's a price to pay for failure. And there's one for happiness and sadness. My goal is to help you pick the right price. You're going to have to work at it, and you're going to have to make some changes, but the changes are so worth it. Life is too short not to be happy, and it's too long not to do well.

The Good Life Rules eliminate frustrations and unhappiness and help you be the same person at work that you are at home. Once those roadblocks are out of the way, you can't help but perform better at work and at home. Your biggest problem is going to be going to sleep at night, because you're going to be so excited about life again.

As much as I enjoy my family, I couldn't spend the time away from them delivering this message if I didn't believe it with all my heart. With five or more presentations to give every week, I suppose it'd be easier to read from a prepared script. But I spend hours personalizing *The Good Life Rules* message for the people who will be sitting in front of me—because the message is too important to let it get lost in some boring, monotone speech.

I have dedicated my life to "building better people"—in my family and in my job. I'm absolutely inspired by that idea. I'm tired of seeing beautiful corporate buildings, magnificent balance sheets, great products, and palatial houses, when the people just look so worn out. That's why companies and groups keep bringing me back—to help people see the important things a little more clearly and to help them fall back in love with where they are. And that's why I've written this book.

It's time to make a change.

At the end of each of the chapters in this book, you'll see a forty-eight-hour action plan—concrete ways you can get started on those changes. Why forty-eight hours? Because life is distracting. And if you don't act on something once you decide to do it, life's distractions start to melt your resolve. The action items are a way to help the points I make in each chapter stick in a meaningful way. Give them a try.

Before we get started, let me make a request, and you might think it's a little bit strange. If you read this book and take something from it that helps you build a better life, I'll be absolutely thrilled—but I don't want you to tell anybody it came from me. As crazy as that sounds—after all, my publishers would be happy to sell as many books as they can—stick with me for a minute.

If you've read this far, you probably have something in your life you want to change. And there are people in your life who love you, who have probably been working on you for a long time to make that change—whether you've noticed it or not. If something I say connects for you, and you go and tell your wife or husband or coworker that you're doing something differently because you read it in a book written by somebody you don't even know, what does that say about the person who has been working on you all that time?

It's happened to me plenty of times. I would listen to a speaker or read a personal development book and rush home to tell my wife how groundbreaking the information was. How I was going to change all these things about my life. Then I'd see tears in her eyes. "Why does it take somebody else to get that message through to you?" she'd ask.

You owe it to yourself and the people around you to build a better you. And you should search for the best ways to make that happen. This book will certainly help you, but the change itself has to come from you.

Do yourself a favor and give the important people in your life all the credit for your transformation. I don't mind if you go buy a couple of extra copies of this book to hand out, but give the credit to the important people in your life. They've been working on you a lot longer than I have. I've just come up with a different way to get through.

Let's get started.

THE
GOOD
LIFE
RULES

Rule

1

The Fundamental Rule: Be Willing to Change

You're here to have The Good Life. That's why we're all here. That's the reason we have careers and build families and try so hard—or at least it should be. But too many people think they can't have it—that they aren't smart enough or talented enough or lucky enough, or that there isn't enough time in the day.

That's just not true.

You can have The Good Life, and I'm going to show you how. Over the course of these pages, I'm going to introduce you to the eight rules for The Good Life—a systematic combination of strategies and techniques that have been working long before you and I were on this earth. I'm just a guy who is helping deliver the message in an organized, inspirational way. I've lived these keys in my own life for more than thirty years, and I've been fortunate that thousands of organizations have trusted me with their most precious resource—their people.

Getting Ready for The Good Life

My basic message for you here is the same one that has inspired sales staffs and reassured employees whose companies were going through tough times. It's the same one my kids have been hearing from me since they could understand my words. Anybody—and I mean anybody—can have The Good Life. You just need to learn the right rules.

Are you tired of feeling like you're just putting in time at your job?

Or maybe you've got some exciting, positive opportunities in front of you, and you want to learn how to better prepare for the changes that are going to come with those new opportunities.

Do you want to feel inspired by what you do again?

Are you just starting out in a new job, and you want to begin with the right attitudes and habits so you can be successful?

Do you want to feel excited when you get home and see your family and have them be excited to see you?

Do you want your energy back?

Are you weighed down by feelings of uncertainty in your job or with your family?

All of these situations and feelings are completely normal and common in a world where our schedules are so crowded with responsibilities and obligations—both the ones we pick and the ones that are picked for us. The thought of wrestling life into a manageable system can certainly be intimidating, especially if you don't know where to start.

That's where The Good Life Rules come in.

And what are those rules? Let me give you a quick look at the map of our entire journey, chapter by chapter. When you see it, I think you'll be excited about where we're headed, and the journey won't seem so daunting. And you'll see why the first rule, the willingness to change, is the battery that makes the entire process work:

The Good Life Rules

1. The willingness to change. Recognizing the need to adapt to what's going on around you. Nothing changes until you change. Once you change, everything changes.

2. The willingness to learn. A step-by-step guide to expanding your knowledge base. Nothing new in, nothing new out.

3. Getting to the why in life: the EAT plan. Training yourself to see new opportunities and understanding how to find the inspiration behind them.

4. The diminishing intent key: getting to why. Learning to act decisively on the important things. Those who focus on the *how* in life always end up working for those who focus on the *why*.

5. Choosing to be faithful. Appreciating what you have before you lose it. Good people appreciate what they have before they lose it. Average people only appreciate those good things once they're gone.

6. Creating new habits. Breaking the cycle of bad habits and replacing them with good ones. We're not looking for New Year's resolutions. We're looking for a new way of living life.

7. Sharing knowledge. Become an effective leader in your life. Don't think you're a leader? You are if somebody's relying on you.

8. Streamlining your life. Learning how to say no. You can't grow in life until you learn to say no.

Once you have learned these rules, you need to put them all together, turning your new changes into lifelong traits. The greatest asset a company has is its people. So if the people grow, the company and the industry will become better places for us to be.

I want to make one promise to you right up front. For each one of these rules, I'm going to give you more than just a bunch of empty words. When people call me a motivational speaker, I wonder what they're talking about, because I don't think that describes me at all. I'm not here to motivate you. Take an idiot and motivate him and you've got a motivated idiot—somebody who's full of energy and activity, but none of it is directed at the tasks that are most important. My job is to inspire you and help you get to where you want to go. I promise to help you understand the *why* behind each of these rules and to give you concrete, specific methods for implementing the keys in your life. Focus on the *how* and you'll be motivated. Focus on the *why* and you'll be inspired.

One basic truth about change is that allowing comfort, procrastination, and fear to convince you to avoid change will leave you with less tomorrow than you have today. You can't stay still on a bicycle. You'll fall over. The easier you are on yourself when nobody is around, the harder life will be on you. The flip side is true, too. Work harder on yourself and life gets easier, and your job starts working for you instead of the other way around. You learn new skills, change the way you make choices—get The Good Life. Change where you're looking and the motivations for what you're doing. Let that anger and those grudges go, so you can grow.

Are You Willing to Change?

Let's start with the willingness to change rule, and I'll show you what I mean.

I think the word *change* is unsettling for a lot of people—especially in business—because it's been used as a code word for things nobody would want to hear. "Changes" in market mean we have to make some "changes" in the organizational structure. Even when the word doesn't mean the potential loss of a job, it can cause some fear. You hear that you have to change because it's good for the company, or change for your career, or change because the world is changing.

In this chapter, I will show you how to take the fear and uncertainty of change and turn it into optimism and enthusiasm. Once you embrace this new attitude, you'll understand that becoming open to change and willing to do things differently puts you in position to choose the direction of those changes. It's the difference between buying a specific ticket for a certain place at the airport and getting on the right plane, or getting shoved into a random Jetway and onto a plane that's going to a place you didn't pick—and didn't pack for.

Deciding What's Important

Let me tell you about an eye-opening experience in my own life to show you what I mean. When I was a kid, growing up in Colorado, my mother kept a house that made the Cleavers' house look completely disorganized. Everything had its place. Of course, when I got married, I just assumed that that was the way things were supposed to be. Early in our marriage, my wife and I both worked, and the kids certainly kept us busy when we got home. I wasn't the kind of dad who came home and expected everything to be done for him—I did my own laundry and the dishes, fed the animals, things like that. I just couldn't stand it when my laundry was on the floor when I got home.

One day, I got home from work and my clothes were pushed into a pile on the floor next to the bed. I just lost it. I went out back, where Margaret was playing with the kids, and I just let her have it. How many times did I have to tell her not to throw my laundry on the floor? Was it too much to ask?

You see, Margaret had gotten home from work and wanted to take a nap. The kids wanted to be with her, so they all piled into the bed. She moved the clothes so they could all fit.

After my blowup, she got tears in her eyes.

"Fine. But you have to make a choice. Do you want me to be a good mom and teach these kids The Good Life? Or do you want me to fold your clothes?" she asked quietly.

And she made me choose, right there.

At that moment, I knew I could be a single guy with a really clean house—and not understand what the Good Life is really all about—or I could have a great wife who would be a great mom to our kids and a great family because I learned to adapt to the people who were important to me.

So you see, fear and greed are what drive change. You're either so fearful of what's going to happen to you—and believe me, the thought of losing my wife and kids was scary—or you're so tempted by what you can have that you do what's necessary to get it. The question is, what are you driven by? If it's fear, be a big boy or a big girl and accept it. If it's greed—you feel like you want a bigger home or a new boat—that's fine, but you have to understand that those motivations are totally different. Fear is looking backward. Greed is looking forward. What is it that is going to inspire you to change?

Positive or negative, change is coming. Who's going to choose it for you? Being a follower is never going to be a recipe for satisfaction. You're called to be the leader of your own life. You're not called to have somebody else decide for you. It's not the government's job to dictate what you do. The number one step toward taking charge of your own life is looking in the mirror and saying,

I'm changing because I want to change. I did this, and it's the reason I have a wife and three great kids.

So many "self-help" books and personal development speakers have tried to give people such easy-to-digest ways to change that the entire subject has almost become a cliché. And to be honest, most of them diminish how important change is—reducing it to some sort of superficial New Year's resolution process that will make you feel better about yourself for a few days or a few weeks.

I'm going to give you my own rules for making a successful change, but I have to stress that understanding *why* change has to happen is more important than the practical steps to achieving it. Becoming a why-focused person—which we're going to talk a lot more about in Chapter 3—is crucial, because that's what generates all the energy and discipline for your efforts. If you're inspired, you're going to be determined to succeed; and then, you can use the specific steps I'm going to show you here to make the process easier.

Getting in the Game

A few years ago, I was the coach of my son Johnathan's soccer team. I had two ironclad rules for the parents when they came to watch their thirteen-year-olds play. First, there was no cussing allowed. Second, you couldn't be a "bad seed" by heckling your kid—or anybody else's—from the stands.

We decided to take the kids to a big weekend tournament down in San Antonio, and it was going really well. The team got to the semifinals, and we were winning that game by two goals in the second half when something terrible happened. One of the dads from our team didn't like a call the sixteen-year-old referee made, and he just unloaded on her from the stands. I was completely shocked by it and more than a little uncomfortable.

Here we were, ready to get to the championship game, but if I let that heckling go, I'd be teaching these kids that the rules matter only if there's nothing on the line.

I walked onto the field and called the referee over. Her name was Lela. I asked her if she could go over and tell the other coach that we were going to forfeit the game. She was stunned and asked me why I'd do something like that, considering the score.

"I didn't come to San Antonio just to win a tournament," I said. "I came here to teach my kids."

I knew I was going to get a lot of grief from those parents. But I decided that I needed to take a strong leadership stand on my sideline.

People forget that life is a game. Spectators are watching, people are on the field with you, and you are responsible for your sideline—there are people who are depending on the choices you make.

You know who understood what I did, completely? The kids. Because they understand when something is consistent. They knew that they could bank on what I said. And I'd been talking about the importance of sportsmanship and respectfulness for the entire season. Who didn't understand? The parents. One dad came to me and said I'd be talking to his lawyer. Another demanded that I pay his expenses for the trip. A mom told me she had already taken a picture next to the trophy.

I had to accept the truth at that moment. If I didn't change where we were, we would repeat where we were going. If I tolerated what happened, it would only get worse at the next tournament game, because the parents would see I didn't mean what I said. I assembled the parents right then, and I said, "If you want these kids to get on the bus with me for a big tournament in Washington, D.C., then you have to show up at the next practice ready to play."

They got all excited, because they thought they were going to play the kids. They went out and bought new shoes and new shorts, and every single one of them showed up at that next practice.

After splitting the parents into teams, I told the kids that practice would be a little different that night. I said the parents were going to play a full-field scrimmage, complete with referees.

Some of the parents looked shocked and told me that this wasn't very funny.

"You're right," I said. "Where we're going with this isn't funny at all."

They started playing, and it was pretty amazing to see the kids transform into the kind of spectators their parents were. Moms and dads were running up and down the field, and you could hear one of the kids yelling, "Run, Dad!" A mom cranked a shot right at an open net and missed over the crossbar. Her son yelled, "Mom! Focus! That could have been the game winner!"

The most memorable image I have from the night is of a parent I call Tiny. He's 350 pounds, at least, and he was gasping as he ran up and down the field behind the play. His favorite thing to yell at his son was always, "Suck it up, man!" What was the first thing the kids yelled when he started to fall behind the action? "Suck it up, man!"

From that day, we never had another problem. Those parents realized that it's really easy to be critical from the sidelines—in soccer and in life—when you're not the one out there playing the game.

What does that have to do with change, you ask?

Six months later, one of the dads stopped at my house with an $8,500 Polaris four-wheeler on a trailer.

"Bryan, I went and bought this for you. I know your kids all have one and you don't, and I thought you should be able to join in," he said, moving to unhook it from the trailer.

"You're right. My four-wheeler went to college instead," I said. "Don't rub it in."

Now, I was pumped. I love my toys, and that was a big toy for me. I was very excited and very thankful. But then it happened. I became very uncomfortable with the gift, and I knew it wasn't right to take it. Temptation seems to show up pretty often when you start living The Good Life Rules. So I requested respectfully (and painfully) that he take it back.

"But wait," he said. "You haven't heard the story."

I told him I couldn't hear the story until he got the four-wheeler out of my sight. Why? Because people can't focus on the good things that come from change, because they're so concerned with what they're going to lose—the fears.

Once he took the four-wheeler back, I said, "I can hear you now."

He said, "You remember when you put me on the soccer field, and I heard my son screaming at me? I learned a lesson that night. I wasn't just screaming on the soccer field. I was screaming at home, too.

"I decided to take some of the advice you'd been giving the team, about acting on things that come into your heart within forty-eight hours. I went home, and I told my wife that I learned a lesson, and I was going to change. She told me she had heard it way too many times, but she said she saw something in my eyes that made her willing to give me a little more time."

One of the biggest mistakes we make in life is that we lose faith and don't give it enough time. Don't lose your faith in The Good Life, and give yourself enough time to get it. That's what she did for him.

He continued his story. Six months go by, and this man and his wife went out to dinner at Three Forks, a fantastic steak house in Dallas, a couple of days before he brought this four-wheeler to my house. Before the food came, she handed him a packet of divorce papers and asked him to look at the date. It was from the day the parents played that soccer game. That was the day he came home and told her about how he was going to change, and she held off to see what would happen. She tore up the papers at that dinner, and she told him he had changed so much that she decided to live the rest of her life with him.

I didn't stop that guy on the soccer field that night and tell him he needed to change his attitude. Once he finished the game, I didn't set out a list of steps for him to get along better with his family. And I'm not the one who saved his marriage. He was just in position to finally see *why* change was important. He got the inspiration—and the willingness—to change. You see, I didn't write this book just for you. I wrote this book for the people who are depending on you. And if you understand that, you understand the *why*.

If you understand why it's important to change your life in these important ways, you're on your way to getting The Good Life. It could be a change in the way you handle your money. It could be a change in the way you deal with your kids. It could be a change in how you deal with your career. It's falling back in love with the good things you have in your life before you lose them.

A few years later, I was giving a talk at Perot Systems, in front of three hundred people, and I told the story of the four-wheeler and the saved marriage. At the end, a woman in the back stood up and said, "I just wanted to say that you might think this is just a story, and Bryan is just trying to make a point. It really happened. I was one of the moms on the field that day. And it saved my marriage, too."

Look Up

Once you develop that willingness to change, you're going to experience something that must be pretty similar to going through eye surgery and being able to see more clearly than you ever have. All of a sudden, you have this perspective on your life—and the things you want to happen in it—that wasn't there before.

One of my sons always talked about how much he loved high school and how it would be hard to leave his friends and go to college. I told him, "You can't stay. You have to grow," and sent him to LSU.

He went off to school, and when he came back home to visit that first year, he went out with some of his friends from high school who hadn't left. When he came back from that first night out, he couldn't stop talking about how glad he was that he had left town and gone to school. He couldn't have imagined what it would have been like to stay.

Why? Because you can't go back. You grow, and you see things differently. More completely. That's what's so powerful about that ability to change. You have to change so you can see that different perspective.

I was coming back home from a trip to the East Coast one time, and I got bumped up to a seat in first class. It was a nice surprise, because I was wiped out from giving two talks that day. I was looking forward to just relaxing for the three-hour flight to Dallas.

In the seat next to me, a lady had her computer and some papers out, and she was engrossed in her work for the first half of the flight. That made me happy, because my voice hurt and I needed some rest. I was getting ready to doze off when she looked up at me and said, out of the clear blue, "My son tells me I need to get out and start dating."

Okay, I'm thinking to myself. I'm uncomfortable. That's quite a way to start a conversation with a stranger.

"Why aren't you dating?" I asked.

"My husband left me, so I buried myself in work," she said. "Besides, who would want to date me?"

"Well, a lot of guys on this plane would," I said. She was an attractive woman, for sure. "Can I offer you some advice?"

She shrugged. "Sure."

Things pop into my head, and I don't know where they come from sometimes, so I said, "Look up. Then, look out. Get outside yourself. You're going to see opportunities that have been staring at you for a long time."

I told her that when she looked up, she was going to see a lot of guys looking back at her.

"Pick one," I said and gave her my card. "Let me know how it turns out."

A few weeks later, she sent me an e-mail: "Thank you for the advice. I looked up, looked out, and saw a lot looking back. I picked one. I'm going out on a date tomorrow."

If you're trying to get to The Good Life and you're walking with your head down, you're missing out. You're not seeing everything. You're not seeing the gold mines all around you. Look up. It might be frightening at first, but trust me, you'll be glad you did. When you're done with this book, one of the most important things I want for you is to be able to walk with your head up, so you can see those Good Life opportunities that have been waiting for you for almost too long. And you'll be ready to pick one.

Evaluate Your Surroundings

When you start looking around, you're going to notice the opportunities I just described, but you're also going to see some things you don't like. You're going to be like the person who buys a fixer-upper house and then takes the first serious tour of the property after the sale closes. You'll see the things you liked about the house—the original crown moldings, the gorgeous view of the lake—but also some not-so-nice things you might not have noticed before, like cracks in the foundation or water damage under the sink.

Think about the people you surround yourself with: coworkers, acquaintances, even friends you've had for a long time. Without a doubt, we all absorb positive and negative traits, habits, and attitudes from the people around us day to day. I'm sure you can look at your roster of friends and immediately pick the ones who have the most sympathetic ear or the ones who are the most fun at a cocktail party—and yes, the ones you don't enjoy spending time with as much as you used to.

One of the sad things about human nature is that when you're having troubles, if you tell a casual acquaintance about it, chances are that person is happy to hear you're unhappy. Why? Because it means that he or she is not the only one who's miserable. That's why the phrase "misery loves company," despite being such a cliché, oftentimes rings so true.

Now, it doesn't take a rocket scientist to figure out that if you're surrounded by negative or angry people, it's going to be harder for you to be a happy, positive person. We're social animals, and there's a powerful subconscious motivation to fit in with the group. For a long time, this was something I knew intuitively, but it was hard to commit to the idea that sometimes even your friends can be bad for you. I'm a very loyal person, and that was a hard step for me to take.

But I did a presentation for a company in San Diego, and I talked to a top salesman there who really made me understand how important it is to take responsibility for the influence friends can have. The company had gathered twenty-five of its top sales-people to talk about a new product launch, and they brought me in to offer some strategies from my Building a Better Salesperson program.

During a team-building exercise, one salesman, Pete, told me about an experience that changed his life. "About ten years ago I heard a speaker, Mike Murdock, say, 'Show me who you are hanging with and I will tell you where you will be ten years from now.'

"From that challenge, I thought about my life and was shocked at what I saw," Pete said. "I was surrounded by unmotivated people who really didn't have any goals or ambitions in life. I was thirty-eight years old. I was working a dead-end job and living paycheck to paycheck. What a wake-up call! I knew exactly where I'd be in ten years. That day, I promised to change the people I was hanging with."

Now Pete was the top salesman in this group of twenty-five, and he probably had on a $1,500 suit and a watch that cost more than my truck. So it was incredible to hear what he said next. "I didn't look right, dress right, or talk right. I lacked people skills and self-confidence. I lived in the wrong part of town, drove an old junker for a car, and generally felt worthless."

He had my full attention at that point.

"I decided that without an education selling would be my best chance to make something of my life. I went to the library and started reading how-to-sell books. I listened to tapes from sales trainers. I slowly worked my way into the sales arena selling several different products. Eventually, I quit my day job and went into full-time commissioned sales. At every assignment, I always went out of my way to make friends with the top salesperson and mimic what that person was doing."

Finally, Pete turned to this room of top salespeople and said, "Thanks to each of you for letting me hang with you."

Pete had made a decision to change and took the first step by changing who the people were in his life. He understood the value of this first key to The Good Life: a willingness to change.

The real truth in business life—and even family life—is that you, the person, have to change and grow. If you don't, the people in your business and family life will start to wonder if they need to make some changes about who they spend time with. And chances are, those won't be changes you'll like.

The Six Steps to Successful Change

Once you understand the *why* and become willing to change, you've taken the biggest, most important step. Next is acting on that decision and moving forward with the change you want to make.

If you're learning to do something new—and for a lot of people, change is something new—it's great to have a recipe or a list of instructions to follow. I've broken the process of change down into six steps. Follow them and you'll be amazed at how powerful your determination to improve will become.

1. **Commit to the change.** It's easy to get bogged down in the mistakes you've made. Let those go so you can grow and commit to doing something different. Write down your goal. Put the paper in a place where you can see it when you get up and go to bed. Even if you slip up a little, you've got to push yourself toward the change goal. I know that's an easy thing to say, but in Chapter 6 I'm going to show you some strategies you've never seen before—like learning to make your addictive personality work for you, instead of against you.

2. Make a no list. In this change process, you're moving away from the behaviors you did before—ones that weren't working. This process is going to involve saying no to your past thoughts, your past choices, and influential people who led you in a different direction. Take the time to write out a list of the things you're going to say no to; then laminate it and carry it in your wallet. In the Appendix, I'll even show you the no list I've got in my wallet right now. As strange as it may sound to you, this is a crucial, crucial step if you're going to make a long-term, positive change. Why? Because you can't add anything to your life without subtracting something to make room. For example, I decided I wouldn't take any speaking engagements that required me to be away from home for more than one night. It's just not worth the cost of being away from my family.

3. Create a plan. Once you've identified the change you want to make, what are the steps you need to take to make it happen? Breaking any assignment up into smaller pieces makes it more manageable. You can achieve little successes along the way, and it makes it easier for you to measure your progress. The act of writing out the plan is empowering, too. It gives you the feeling that you understand the full scope of what you're doing, and that you're ready for the challenge.

4. Ask for help. If you needed to go out in your backyard and dig a hole, you'd basically need a shovel and enough time to get it done. If the change you're making is a simple one, maybe a shovel and some time are enough. But for a more formidable or complicated challenge, don't be afraid to ask for help. If you were going to rewire the electricity in your house and you didn't know a thing about how to do it, you'd call an electrician. Asking for help also can do two important things. First, it can give you perspective. Some elements of the change might not be as challenging as you think, and an expert can point out ways to save time and effort. We'll be talking about this in Chapter 7. Second, talking to somebody you trust can help you feel like you've got some support. If you're trying to lose weight, telling your spouse about it will hopefully keep the suggestions to go out and eat pizza to a minimum. A trusted confidante can also give you a poke when you're slipping.

5. Execute. Take the written plan you put together and refer to it every day, just like you'd read a map to figure out how to get around in a new town. My son's goals are tied to having access to his truck. If he accomplishes them, he gets his truck. He can always choose to do something—like get a tattoo—if he's willing to trade it for his truck. Looking at his printed list reminds him of the choices every day. Another critical element of the execution step is getting an honest assessment of your progress. That's something you can track yourself, but hearing from a close friend or a spouse is valuable, too.

6. Celebrate. Changing is hard, and it can certainly be stressful. When you get to where you want to be with a change, that's a cause for celebration. And when I say celebrate, I mean do something special—in proportion to the level of change, of course. If it was a big change, don't just give it a toast with a glass of wine. Get away for a weekend, or pick something else extraspecial that you wouldn't otherwise do. Treating yourself like this at the end also motivates you for the next change.

And if there's one thing we've learned so far, it's that there's always another change, right?

At the end of every chapter, I'll give you a set of four or five "homework assignments" for the first forty-eight hours after you read the chapter, to help you get started living The Good Life Rules.

Forty-Eight-Hour Action Plan

1. Find your most important no. We talked about making a no list in this chapter. Start by picking the thing you most want to eliminate from your life and make it number one on that new list. Maybe you'd rather spend more time with your kids on the weekends, so you say no to cutting the grass and pay a neighborhood kid to do it instead.

2. Draw a home/work line. There's a bridge over a creek a mile from my house, and whenever I'm headed home, I promise myself to let my work go when I cross that bridge. I fully separate work and family time. Pick a landmark near your house that works as the dividing line between work and home.

3. Get an honest assessment. Ask the person closest to you aside from a spouse or child—somebody who doesn't live with you—to give you a pull-no-punches personal critique. Make it clear that you want to know what things in your life you're really great at and which things could use improvement. Some of it may be painful, but it will hopefully give you some fresh perspective.

4. Pick a replacement addiction. We all have bad habits. People automatically come with addictive personalities. I'm not asking you to kick smoking or give up red meat in a weekend. Start small. Within forty-eight hours, pick a small habit you want to break and find a replacement activity for it. I was starting to gain some weight, so I changed my eating schedule from three regular meals to four smaller meals, so I could go through each day eating less food without feeling hungry.

Rule

2

Be a Learner

You've made a tremendous commitment to The Good Life by showing a willingness to change. Now it's time to lay some of the building blocks on that foundation.

The world is a big place. There's so much out there to do and see—and so many ways to get offtrack if you're not watching where you're going. Now that you're ready to reach for The Good Life, it's important to learn how to find the information that not only points you in the right direction, but makes the journey easier and more enjoyable, too. It's time to *learn how to learn*.

That might sound silly, but a great many people struggle every day because they don't know how to do just that. They aren't open to new information and experiences, so the idea of changing just freaks them out completely. Then they either make rushed, bad decisions or they just freeze and hope their problems go away.

You don't have to be one of those people.

In this chapter, I'm going to tell you some inspiring stories about people who learned how to learn. You're going to see how soaking up new information will contribute to your being a good family member or a good employee. And I'm going to help you ingrain the habit of reading—and learning—in a few simple-to-follow steps.

How a Book Can Change Your Life

If you're wondering how I can understand and sympathize with the person who's struggling to open up to the idea of learning, let me tell you a story to give you some perspective.

When I was in high school and college, my learning process involved sitting at the table with a book in front of me, going over the same page for thirty minutes. I had a classic case of attention-deficit/hyperactivity disorder (ADHD), which meant I had all the energy in the world—but only a ten-second attention span. So every reading assignment was like a mental fistfight for me. I'd get to the end of a chapter, then realize that I had already read it. I was concentrating so hard on the physical process of reading that I wasn't absorbing the information I needed.

When I got out of school, I took a job as a salesman because, honestly, it was a profession that seemed not to require a lot of reading and studying.

The problem was, I sucked as a salesman. I was willing to do all the dirty work, cold-calling and driving all over the place to try to make connections, but I didn't know what I was doing in terms of closing sales. I made a lot of friends, but I wasn't making any money. Lucky for me, my wife, Margaret, was a teacher. She kept pounding into my head the idea that I could use books to learn and get better at what I was doing. Even if I didn't enjoy reading—and honestly, to this day it's not something I'd put on my list of things I love to do—I gained a great respect for what reading and learning could do for my career. It helped me quit making the same mistakes over and over again.

But it took somebody else's crisis for me to really understand the power of Rule 2 in my own life, and the lives of others.

My mentor at my first job was an older guy named Jerry. He and I had a lot in common. We came in early, stayed late, and enjoyed talking about a lot of the same things, like football and horses. Jerry took me under his wing and gave me my first education in the art of selling. I was like a sponge, listening and learning about how to figure out what customers wanted and needed, and how to close the sale.

Jerry arrived at his twenty-fifth year with the company, and he was looking forward to the standard recognition that usually came with that milestone: the company president would come by and make a speech, and all the salesmen in the division would be there to offer congratulations. It was obviously a big moment in his life.

We all assembled in this hotel conference room in Des Moines, Iowa, on the big day, ready for the president to come in and shake Jerry's hand. The door opened, and you could see how excited Jerry was. Heck, I was, too, because he was like a father to me.

But instead of the president of the company coming in, a guy we had never seen before stuck his head in. "I'm flying through town, and I'm supposed to drop something off for Jerry," he said.

Jerry raised his hand, and the guy walked over and handed him a little box. "Congratulations on twenty-five years with the company," he said, and turned and walked out of the room.

We all crowded around Jerry to see what was in the box. He opened the lid, and inside was a watch. Not a gold watch, but a gold-painted watch, with a cheap engraving.

Jerry tried his best not to get angry, but he just crumbled. He had worked so hard for the company. He had given it his all, for his entire professional life. Jerry had tied up so much of his self-worth in the company, and achieving this milestone, that when it wasn't what he had hoped—when the company didn't give back the way he expected—he was crushed.

That night, I watched Jerry drown his sorrows at the hotel bar, and I was worried about him—enough so that I stayed with him. The next morning, I got up and thought to myself, "What can I do?"

I took a walk outside the hotel, past a bookstore, and I saw a copy of Norman Vincent Peale's *The Power of Positive Thinking* in the window. I had heard that that book had helped Lou Holtz, the Notre Dame football coach, so I thought I'd get it and maybe it would help Jerry, too. Honestly, I didn't know what else to do.

I bought the book, took it back to my room, and scanned it. Then I walked over to Jerry's room and gave him the book. I told him, "You mean the world to me, Jerry. I don't know how to help you, but I thought this book might. All I know is that life's not over. There's more to it than this, and you have to keep going."

Jerry called me two days later, and I had never heard him so happy. He said, "Bryan, I read that book you gave me, and it was so freeing. I spent so much time concentrating on working for the company that I forgot to work on myself. I forgot to get myself right so that the company could work for me."

Over the next two years, Jerry set sales records that still haven't been broken. He sold everything there was to sell. He left the company and went to work for another one, and he set records there, too. As far as I know, he never did retire.

It just blew me away that somebody could be inspired to make such a dramatic change in his life simply from learning something new—something that to the average person might seem trivial because it just came from "some book." I also learned a valuable lesson about understanding what really matters in life.

It's not that Jerry shouldn't have been disappointed about the way the company treated him. He should have been, because it was pretty shabby. But if he had been learning and developing as a person *outside* of who he was as a salesman all that time, he would have been able to put that distasteful event in its proper perspective when it happened. He'd have seen what we all saw—that he was a great friend, mentor, *and* salesman—no matter what his anniversary watch was made out of. He would have had that balance we're all looking for.

My experience with Jerry that day made me understand that you should never underestimate the power of keeping your mind open to new information. If you're always receptive, you could gain just that piece of the puzzle you need, when you're least expecting it. Seeing Jerry's transformation changed the way I learned and read—from the process I used to my motivation for doing it. I'll tell you more about that later in this chapter, but first let me introduce you to Michelle and Herby.

Learning Your Way to a New Career

Some of the benefits that come from reading great books are obvious. A book changed my friend Jerry's life forever. I've got my own list of books than have been game-changers for me, too. (I've listed them in Recommended Reading starting on page 171, or you can visit BryanDodge.com.) Books allow you to pick up strategies and information that can directly help with situations in your own life. For example, if you were a customer service representative for a cell phone company and I suggested that reading the literature on the latest phones in your company's lineup would be a good idea, you wouldn't be too surprised by that advice.

But some of the benefits of learning are a little more subtle. Reading more books, magazines, and newspapers gives you so much more potential common ground with the people you meet. Being a learner makes you more interesting, more open to new information and new challenges. Having a broad perspective allows you to share the same "language" of common experience and allows you to feel more comfortable with people more quickly. If you're not a reader, your world will stay pretty small. You won't have as many "connecting points" with other people.

I met a woman named Michelle, who had put in twenty years as an accountant in the pension and retirement business. She had always wanted to get involved in law and wondered if a law degree might be the next step in her career.

Michelle did some research and found a one-year program where she could get a paralegal certificate while still working full time at her accounting job. She finished the program and, because of her varied business experience, was quickly recruited by a prestigious national law firm with a local office in her town. She had the job of her dreams, and she didn't even have to relocate.

But six months later, Michelle's world collapsed. Her new law firm lost a major client, and they laid off their most recent hires. Michelle was out of work.

Then Michelle's husband reminded her about the time he had been laid off, telling her, "It was the best thing that ever happened to me. It put me in position to go after something I love to do."

Michelle was hurting, but she decided to try to adopt her husband's positive attitude and learn how to make her accounting experience and new paralegal credential work for her. Her husband suggested she apply for a job at the government agency where he worked, and even though the salary was half of what she had been making, Michelle saw it as a chance to use her experience in a new way.

She interviewed for the position—as an auditor—and got it and plunged into learning the ropes. Michelle had had more than twenty years of experience working on the other side of the table from IRS and commercial accounting firms auditors. Now, she *was* one of the auditors, which was certainly an adjustment. But her accounting experience and legal background was a perfect match for the job.

A year and a half later, one of the government agencies Michelle was auditing had a problem with one of its pension plans. Michelle and a colleague came up with a solution for that problem and presented it to the agency directors. She ended up saving the agency a tremendous amount of money and time and was invited to give her presentation at a national conference. There, she got national exposure for her ideas—all because she used what she knew and worked hard to become familiar with some complicated government pension and retirement audit regulations. In fact, I met Michelle at that very conference.

Since that time, Michelle has gone on to big things—promotions, and a salary much bigger than the one she was nervous about losing as a paralegal. She was able to achieve these things because she was willing to learn, and willing to take what some people might see as adversity and use it to grow into a better place.

Sometimes, you lose control in your life, by losing a job or going through some other difficult situation, like Jerry did. One way to regain that control is to focus on an element in your life that you *can* change, like Michelle did. Regaining control of a part of your life like that helps you regain a sense of equilibrium.

Breaking Out of a Holding Pattern

Of course, you don't necessarily have to go through a traumatic job loss to be able to use the advice I'm talking about here. Many of us start a job and do it well for twenty or thirty years. The ability to do that is a compliment to both the employee and the employer, for building a great relationship. But with such a long-term relationship comes challenges for both, too.

If you're that employee with twenty years of service, are you going to be repeating what you've been doing all that time, or are you going to keep growing during your twenty-first year? I've seen statistics that say a person is in a growing mode for the first five years of a job, then spends the next ten years consolidating that knowledge and getting very efficient at the job. But what you do after that period says everything about who you are as an employee. After fifteen years, if you stop growing, that becomes a burden on your employer, and the company may make a change, or you may get frustrated and move on yourself and go through that learning process all over again.

As I said in the last chapter, it's not that you want to avoid change. It's that you want to be in control of the direction it takes. Increasing your knowledge base helps you stay in control of that direction.

When I spoke at a jeweler's association meeting in Oklahoma, I met a jewelry store manager named Herby, who pulled me aside after my talk to tell me his story. Herby had had some personal struggles in his life that had sucked a lot of his enthusiasm out of his work. He actually said he sometimes wished he could return his paycheck to his boss with a note of apology, because he felt like he wasn't holding up his end of the deal.

One day, Herby's boss took him aside and put his arm around him. He said he understood what Herby was going through. He even gave Herby a book that had been influential in his own early career.

Herby decided then that he needed to be more thankful about where he was—in an organization with a supportive manager and a family-type atmosphere—and he needed to commit to being more open to learning. He asked his boss to show him how to be more helpful to customers, and he decided at that moment that he was going to stop being so concerned about his long-term career plans and instead focus on getting the best customer-satisfaction marks he could for one month.

You probably know where I'm headed with this. When Herby became more open to learning how to be a better salesman and improved his attitude, his gift for the job was revealed. He went from being in danger of losing his job to being the number one salesman in the company. Within a year, he had earned a series of promotions to manager, which earned him a trip to the conference where I was speaking. Focusing on developing his skills got him where he wanted to be in his career in a fairly short time, when years of unproductive worrying had almost gotten him fired.

It's Not Just About You

We've spent some time talking about some success stories, and that's all fine and good. It's certainly inspiring to hear about people who have been able to grow that willingness to learn in their lives. But even if you don't buy into what I'm saying about learning or reading to help yourself on the job, you can find a different motivation to be a continuous learner.

If you don't feel like reading for yourself, read for other people. Taking the time to read a book and decide that it's important enough to share with somebody you care about is a gift (which is why you shouldn't just hand somebody a book and walk away).

I've been hearing all the reading advice from this chapter for years, but from different sources. My dad told me I was never going to get anywhere unless I was a reader. I had professors all through school who tried to get me interested in different books, but it never "took." In fact, I went to a graduation party after my last year at Nebraska, and I vividly remember telling one of my favorite professors that I was so glad to be done with school because I never had to read a book again. He gave me this great deadpan look, and said, "So this is as good as you're going to get?"

My ADHD was certainly part of my troubles. As I said, reading was hard for me, and my attention span wasn't (and isn't) very long. My wife, Margaret's, patience as a teacher has had just about everything to do with where I am today, and I became a reader with her help. But my experience with my friend Jerry is what really motivated me to change from a guy who read grudgingly, because I had to try to keep up, to a guy who reads two or three books a week.

When Jerry responded to that copy of *The Power of Positive Thinking* I gave him, I said to myself, "A book did that for my friend. Now, I know why I need to read. I need to read more so I can help more."

Reading for myself—for entertainment—doesn't inspire me. I fall asleep. But if I read something that I think could interest my wife, or help a friend, I'm all over it. My goal is to give away three thousand books a year to friends, colleagues, family members, and even strangers through my seminars. My mission is to find books that will help people—but I won't give a book to somebody that I haven't read myself.

How do I keep the drive to do that, even when it cuts into time I'd otherwise have for "fun" things? If you have kids, or a spouse, or a significant other, you do things for them that you'd never do for yourself. It's the power of giving, and the power of generosity. Use those powers to inspire your life. The minute you figure out that you can influence people by making the choice to learn, it will flip a switch inside you. You'll find a whole new source of energy you never knew you had.

Inscribe something inside the book you give. The recipient knows who the author is, but when he or she is reminded of who gave it, the book becomes a little treasure. And don't stop there. In the books I give to my family, friends, and business associates, I mark a passage halfway through with a little note that says, "Call me when you get here. We'll have lunch and talk about it." It shows that you took the time to find something you really thought was important. It shows you care about that person. It also inspires the person receiving the book to follow through with reading.

A good book is a "good seed." If you give a book to somebody and they get something from it, they can pass it on to others. That good intention gets spread exponentially. Hey, we all know *how* to read. Having one more reason *why* to read, beyond what's going to help you day to day with family and work, is positively golden.

And as you go through the process of reading to figure out what books are going to help others, what happens? You're absorbing all the information yourself. You've read all the books. But doing it for other people is going to give you more from the experience than you would get if you were doing it for some kind of assignment, or for entertainment.

I have to say one more thing before we get to some of the actual steps you can take to improve your learning habit. And if nothing else I've said here connects, I implore you to consider this point, especially if you have young children: Your kids will do what they see you do. If reading—and learning—isn't important to you, it's not going to be important for them. When you make the choice to be a learner for yourself, you're also making it for them.

When my kids were small, they were like a lot of kids. They liked certain stories, and they wanted me or my wife to read them over and over and over. Whenever my eyes started to glaze over because I knew *exactly* where The Wild Things were or what Curious George was going to do next, I remembered how important it was to grow that thirst for information in my kids. I always wanted reading and learning to be fun for them. That snaps me to attention—and gives me the energy to be a leader for them—to this day.

How to Become a Real Reader

In most of my corporate presentations, I schedule time at the end of the session for question-and-answer. When I've hit hard on the theme we're talking about here—on becoming a willing learner by being a more active reader—I'll almost always get a frazzled response from a person who says he or she just doesn't have enough time in the day to read.

I don't want to downplay real concerns about spending enough time with family or on work, but the lack-of-time excuse just doesn't stand up.

What if I told you that reading twelve books a year would put you in the top 25 percent of all readers in the world? It's true. The average person read one book last year. And if you've learned anything from me so far, it's that I don't want you to be average.

Time isn't the problem when it comes to reading—and learning. Getting started, and starting the habit, is. Let me give you three simple steps to wiring the reading (and therefore the learning) habit into your life, and you'll be ready to reap the benefits.

Find Fifteen Minutes

That's all I'm asking. That might sound like forever if you're just not interested in reading, but trust me, once you get started, it will go by so quickly. If you can find fifteen minutes a day, you can read twenty books in a year. Over five years, you will have read sixty books. If you pick books that pertain to your career—or the career you want to have—how much of an advantage are you going to have over the person who only read three, or is majoring in television?

Pick a Place

Once you've committed to reading for fifteen minutes a day, pick a dedicated spot at home—or even at the lunch table at your office—that becomes your reading spot. More than once, I've been in the home of a very successful person and gone to sit down in a chair, only to be told to pick a different one. People can be particular about their reading chair! Usually, it's the one with the precarious stack of books and magazines next to it.

Because I spend so much time on the road, I don't want to take time away from my wife, kids, and animals when I'm home, so I'll rarely pick up a book then. But when I get on a plane, I'll compose all the e-mails I'm going to need to send out when I land, then pull out a book and go at it until the flight lands.

If you're going to designate a reading chair in your home, follow these rules: Nobody sits in it but you. You can't watch television from it, or eat when you're sitting in it. And you can't drink alcohol when you're there. Do it right and you'll have an heirloom to leave for your children—the place you consistently went to grow. There's a reason why reading chairs of famous people in history have been some of the most expensive antiques you can buy. People understand that such a chair is more than just a piece of furniture.

Know When to Say When

When I talk about reading books, I'm also referring to all the other ways a person can pick up information—magazines, the Internet, newspapers. And because it's easier than ever to have a constant flood of information coming your way, through wireless laptops, cell phones—even the magazine stand at the airport—it can be tough to know when to take a break. I've got engineer buddies who spend twenty hours a day in front of the computer, first on work and then online, chatting with colleagues about engineering *stuff.* You can't be that way, either. That's no better than sitting in front of the television for seven hours a day, from the minute you get home from work.

Remember, *people*—and I mean in-person, not online—are a critical component to this process, too. You're expanding your knowledge base with books and other printed information, but if you aren't taking the time to interact with other people to see how the information plays in the real world, you're missing the point! The human interaction is what will give you the feedback you need to analyze what you're reading next time you crack open a book.

Now, with a willing, open mind, you're ready to take the next big step and apply these skills to claiming The Good Life!

Forty-Eight-Hour Action Plan

1. Go to a bookstore or magazine shop and buy a magazine you've never read before. It should be about a subject that interests you, but completely outside of your business or current hobbies. Surprise your brain for less than five bucks.
2. Substitute a book on tape for the radio during your commuting drive.
3. Set your alarm clock for thirty minutes earlier, and commit fifteen minutes of that time to reading.

4. Make a list of interesting things you learn each day. For example, I'm learning to fly a helicopter. The day I'm writing this chapter, I learned that an airplane's design is such that if you leave the controls alone, the plane *wants* to fly. A helicopter's design is such that if you let the controls go, it wants to fall. But if you have a light touch with it, you can have more control in a helicopter than any other machine.

5. Pick something fun—and active—to learn. Whether it's learning to cook a steak or ride a motorcycle, try something that excites you and gives you a break from your everyday routine.

Rule

3

Get to the Why in Life, or the EAT Plan

Now that you've read the first two chapters, I'm sure you've noticed how important I think it is to be open and receptive to both change and new information. And I'm hoping you've decided that those things are important to you, too, and that you're going to stay with me on this journey.

One of the seductive traps we all can fall into when it comes to change is getting wrapped up in the *how* versus the *why* in life. Just look at how many how-to books, videos, and television programs have been popular over the last few years. They offer to simplify your life with basic how-to steps for fixing a meal, planting a garden, organizing your finances, or even being happy.

If you're a baby boomer, like I am, you're getting to an age where you start to have a few more physical problems—sore knees after a day on the golf course, or an eyeglasses prescription that gets a little stronger all the time. You don't have as much energy as you once did, or maybe your memory is slipping a little. You're saying to yourself, "How can I stay in the game? How can I stay around to enjoy everything I worked so hard for?"

Maybe you start working out, or drinking energy drinks, or you get a prescription that's supposed to be some magic elixir for all your problems. But nothing's working.

Why not? Because those how-to books and videos—and all that effort for effort's sake—miss the point. I'm not saying the information in a how-to book is worthless, it's just incomplete. Chasing the how in life by itself, you're not seeing the big picture. It's like hunting rabbits without a gun. You might catch one, but you won't know what to do with it when you get it.

You've worked hard all these years, eaten the right foods, and exercised to stay in shape. You've helped your kids with their homework and gone to all their games. Now, you're in your golden years, and what was it all for?

I hope that when you ask that question, your answer comes easily.

It's about the journey.

Is that a cliché? Maybe, but it's the truth. You're here to live your life, to enjoy the ride, to cherish the people around you. How you live your life only matters in the context of why you do what you do. So many people feel empty because they've always mindlessly followed instructions—this is how you should organize your career, or this is how you should put together your finances. They've taken the *how* information—which is valuable in its own way—but used it without understanding *why* they're doing whatever it is they're doing. There's no inspiration behind any of it. It's no wonder you see so many people going through life as if it's a series of trips to the DMV that there's no way to get out of.

If you truly want to understand The Good Life Rules, you need to embrace the why. The how is comforting because it's a concrete reminder of what happens next. But the why is the inspiration.

I've spent more than twenty years talking to corporate America, and I can tell the difference between a how-motivated group and a why-motivated group after being behind the podium for five minutes. I can even break down the different groups in a larger crowd. The people who are focusing on the how always end up working for the people who are focusing on the why. The ones who focus on how are looking to be motivated, while the ones focusing on why want to be inspired. Motivation comes and goes. Inspiration is for good.

Let me help you get to the why, and be inspired.

Adding *Why* to Your Vocabulary

Do you have a three-year-old at home? If you don't, you probably did at one time, or you're close to somebody who did. Think about what it was like to have a conversation with that three-year-old. I'm sure it was equal parts charming and frustrating.

What is the most common word in a three-year-old's vocabulary—after the word *no*? Without a doubt, it's "why." Why is the sky blue? Why does a leopard have spots? Three-year-olds try to figure out the world around them, and asking why questions is the most direct way to do it.

Now, the challenges you deal with in your life are more complex than a three-year-old's, but I'd argue that they're just as important, relatively speaking. The world can be just as confusing and scary for a forty-year-old as it is for a three-year-old. And a three-year-old in a good home might have more people to count on for unbiased information, at that.

So why do some of us stop asking why?

I ask this question in almost every presentation I give. I say that I can determine how open a person's mind is in ten minutes or less, just by listening to the number of times the word *why* comes up in the conversation.

And I'm sad to report that it doesn't come up very often. I believe that's because many people are afraid of revealing how much they don't know, either because they're afraid of being criticized, or because they'll feel foolish.

When you ask why, you are vulnerable. But you've also signaled to your brain that it's time to pay attention. Your brain is wired to search for context in all the information you take in. It turns out we're *designed* to ask why questions and apply the answers to the world around us.

Unfortunately, many of us outgrew that why phase and passed into a world where we were taught to learn in a how-to way instead. I see the worst of it in organizations where their people don't have any pride in the business because they can't share in the why of it. I've seen managers manage by saying, "It's not important for you to understand why customer satisfaction is important. Just follow this script and make it happen." That certainly doesn't make for a satisfying work life, yet people live their entire lives that way—sleepwalking through life and following a script somebody else wrote.

Don't get trapped that way.

Avoid the Four Why Traps

I'm not going to kid you. Living by The Good Life Rules takes some effort and practice. The four Why Traps I'm going to describe here are so common in today's world that you'll have to develop some fancy footwork to sidestep them. But don't get discouraged. The Good Life Rules are about building a better life, not a perfect one, or even an "easy" one, like some people try to sell you. The goal here is to get you growing in a consistently positive direction, and to help prepare you for the challenges we all inevitably have to face.

1. Distraction. The number-one way to get lost in the how of life instead of the why is by being distracted—or overwhelmed—by its day-to-day responsibilities. How many times have you said to yourself, "I'm just trying to get through today"? When you get that distracted, overwhelmed feeling, it's difficult to focus on anything more than the next thing on your to-do list.

2. Complacency. It's so very easy to be lazy. Sometimes, laziness is good. After all, is there anything better than finishing some big assignment at work or chore at home and taking a weekend day to relax, watch a ball game, and drink a beer, or sit out in the sun on the patio and take a nap? Of course not, and I'm not suggesting you feel guilty about taking time for yourself like that. It's when laziness turns into a permanent habit—complacency—that you've got a problem. You're complacent when you feel like nothing much is going to change in your life even if you make an effort, so there's no reason to try. It's basically giving up—letting go of the steering wheel and hoping somebody else grabs it to keep from crashing. We're going to talk a lot more about this in Chapter 6.

3. Arrogance. This is a tough one, because it impacts a lot of people who are otherwise high achievers. You can lose sight of the important why questions in life if you get too caught up chasing a career goal. When you've had some successes—raises, promotions, praise from the boss—you can get to feeling you're beating the world. It's great to feel the confidence that comes from success, but if you think you know everything, think again. The kind of cockiness that can come from success has a distinct downside. It makes you unreceptive to fresh ideas, and it can make you unpopular with the people around you.

4. Fear. The most basic barrier to getting to the why is the most visceral one. We all have fear of the unknown. You're taking less of a risk when you follow somebody else's plan, because you're essentially transferring responsibility to that person if it doesn't work out. You can say, "Hey, I was just doing what Bob told me to do." Except, of course, life doesn't work that way. You can get advice from your parents, your friends, your spouse, or even me, but in the end, the choices you make are yours. If you're going to celebrate the successes or mourn the failures, they should at least be from choices *you* made.

Did you recognize yourself in any of those traps? It's okay if you did. We all step in a hole every once in awhile. The key is understanding the how and why of seeing the holes before you step in and getting out of them if you *do* get stuck.

I've developed a philosophy that does just that. It's called EAT. It stands for Eager, Argue, and Thankfulness. It's the simplest way I've found to get to the why in life. Let me tell you a little more about it.

Eager

The first component of EAT, **E**ager, is pretty simple. It's having the open mind we talked about in the first two chapters. It's adding the word *why* back into your vocabulary, like the three-year-old. That openness to learning is essentially working the muscle that is your brain. And just like exercising your biceps or quads, exercising your brain gets it working more efficiently and into better shape.

When you have that receptiveness, you can catch messages when you aren't expecting them. I found my own why in life in a most unexpected place. I'll tell you more of Kate's story in the next chapter, but I can share a few lines of it here because it really illustrates the point I'm trying to make.

Kate, a high school–age girl in our town, passed away suddenly from an undiagnosed illness, and the outpouring of grief was just incredible. I was familiar with her and friendly with her family, and I went to the funeral just like hundreds of other people. I was sitting in the back of the church, and one of Kate's teachers walked over to me. She asked me if I'd be willing to pass on her story about Kate—who had been her favorite student. She had been thinking about Kate in the weeks before she passed away, but had gotten distracted and hadn't found time to call and check in. She never got her chance, and she was just torn up with regret.

At first, I hesitated. I wasn't Kate's dad, or a member of her family. I was just a friend. But this teacher's simple request—for me to share the story in my talks, so that other people wouldn't be too late reconnecting—ended up becoming one of my primary inspirations for doing what I do. It gets me on planes three or four times a week—when I hate to fly. And it pushes me late at night when I'm exhausted, but I need to get a presentation ready for the next morning.

It's the whys in life that can inspire you this way—not the sense of obligation toward a job or a deadline, or the money that comes in a paycheck or commission. The whys can rekindle your fire. If you aren't making the conscious decision to be receptive to what's going on around you—and to be eager to hear things that can teach and motivate you—you're making a mistake.

Everything that happened in that church lined up for me to hear the story—that you need to do what comes into your heart before it's too late—and to share it with hundreds of thousands of people. It's why I place so much value on being an eager listener wherever I go. I know that at any time I could run into somebody who could change my life for the better and teach me something I didn't know.

Argue

The second component, **Argue**, always makes the audience laugh when I bring it up in a presentation. "Hey, one out of three isn't bad," somebody will joke. It's because most people think they're naturally good at arguing.

Actually, what most people are naturally good at is yelling, which is completely different than what I'm talking about here. I don't want you to start screaming at the people who are important to you. I want you to understand that disagreement can be productive. It can help you learn, and learning to deal with disagreement and to resolve issues in an efficient way is a critical step to living The Good Life. It puts you back in control, instead of letting your struggles control you.

My parents strongly believed that any arguments they had should be behind closed doors, away from the kids. They had good intentions, for sure, and they presented a united front to me and my brother and sister, but I lost out on some important lessons because of it.

I never learned how to resolve conflict in a healthy way, and it took marrying into Margaret's family, with all the jockeying and arguing that goes with being one of eight kids, to give me a great model for healthy debate. I saw that Margaret could argue with her brother and sisters or her parents—and even yell at them—but it didn't mean anybody loved anybody else any less. They showed me that you can disagree with someone's point but not make the argument personal. It's even okay to argue vociferously for your cause and in the end agree to disagree.

I'm not embarrassed to say that Margaret has taught me the art of debating—and now I can do it with the best of them. We have had our share of arguments, but knowing what I know about those disagreements, and how productive it was to get everything out in the open, I can't help but shake my head in disbelief when a person tells me he or she's never had an argument with a spouse.

That's a serious red flag.

Why? Because if you aren't sticking up for what you believe, then you aren't doing your spouse any favors in the long run. If both people are clear about what they want and need—and can communicate it without the argument getting mean-spirited and personal—then both people win, no matter what the ultimate resolution is. You've got to be able to get things that bother you out in the open. If there's never any discussion or argument about what's going on in the house, then one person is giving up too much. It's going to be very, very difficult for either person in that relationship to be happy.

It's obvious why this point is important in the scheme of things when it comes to your relationship with your spouse. But why is developing the Argue "muscle" important when it comes to the rest of your life?

Because you need to be able to address the issues and problems in your life before they grow and overtake you completely. You need to stand up for what you know is right and establish what you believe in, so you aren't susceptible to falling for just anything that comes along.

Let me ask you a simple true-or-false question: As you become more successful in life, you'll face more day-to-day challenges—true or false?

It's absolutely true, by any measure.

If you've got more responsibility in your job, or you grow to own your own company, you're going to be facing more challenges every day and making more decisions. When you get married and have children, you're going to be very excited about those great developments, but I can promise you you're going to have more to do and more to worry about when it happens. People who say, "I wish I didn't have any problems" are essentially wishing they were dead.

Life isn't always going to be easy, no matter how hard you wish for it. If you're caught up in that fantasy, you need to get over it. We all have problems now, and more are coming whether we like it or not. The goal is to develop better skills to deal with those problems in a less stressful way.

By understanding the role that the Argue muscle plays in your life, you're going to be able to take each challenge in your life and resolve it in my absolute favorite time frame: on its time. By the words *on its time*, I mean, *when it happens*, because when you meet a challenge as you're faced with it, you're in control of it and how it gets solved. There's only one other choice, and that's to ignore a problem and hope it goes away. But do unaddressed problems just go away? No. They only get worse. And worse than that, by allowing a problem to hang over you, you've let it move into *your* time. Now who does it control? You.

You know why people aren't able to truly live? They let so many things that don't matter gain too much control over their life. Every year at tax time, I watch the news and see the stories of people scrambling to fill out their paperwork in the lobby of the post office and hurry to get the envelope postmarked before midnight on the deadline day. Tax day comes like clockwork every year, and there's no reason not to have things organized ahead of time, so the deadline isn't hanging over you. Even if you're going to owe taxes, you can fill out the paperwork in February and plan for the financial hit in your budget. But some people procrastinate and have that worry in the back of their minds for months. You can't have The Good Life if you leave problems unresolved.

Last year, I had as a guest on my weekly radio show Charlie "Tremendous" Jones. Charlie is a prominent author and speaker, and he distributes a series of popular business books through his ExecutiveBooks.com organization. Charlie told some of the stories from his *Life Is Tremendous* bestseller, and the phones just lit up with people inspired by what he was saying. During the last commercial before Charlie was scheduled to leave, I asked him if he'd be willing to talk about his battle with cancer. He refused and said, simply, "I will live longer if I'm focused on helping others have a good life. That's what I want more than anything else."

Charlie showed me that even if the challenges facing you are significant, if you deal with them directly and resolve to be positive about them, you're going to have The Good Life.

Thankfulness

The final component of the EAT philosophy, Thankfulness, is the one that's been reinforced in me over and over again for thirty years. And I'm not talking about all that blue-sky, green-grass, just-happy-to-be-alive stuff you'd read in some sappy greeting card. I'm talking about developing a true appreciation for the things you have before you lose them.

Have you ever heard somebody say that the grass is greener on the other side of the fence? We all have. But is it? No. They have their own manure over there. They just hide it better. The reason it looks better over there is because that's where you're spending all your time looking. Concentrate more on where you are than where you're not, and on things you can control and not things you can't. It's your choice.

That's easy to say, of course. And it's more than just a matter of snapping your fingers to make it happen. But I have plenty of experience with remarkable people who have put their money where their mouth is, so to speak.

A few years ago, I got a call from a man who was the president of a large software company outside of Dallas.

"My partner said you're the weirdest guy he's ever met," Wayne said. This was a strange way to open a conversation, but since some of my presentations can be over the top, I let it slide. "He also said that if anybody could help us, it'd be you."

I asked him to tell me his problem.

"I've got twenty-five hundred employees walking out of my company."

I asked him how many employees he had.

"Twenty-five hundred."

Someone had raided the company's 401(k) fund and stolen the retirement money of all the employees in the organization. The business was on the ropes, and the employees were ready to walk out the door en masse. The president asked everyone to stay for one more day, so they could at least listen to me.

When I walked into the company's large conference center, you could have cut the tension in the air with a chain saw. Those people were ready to tear me limb from limb if I walked up there preaching the company line. The last thing they wanted was a motivational speaker, and that was the last thing they got.

I told them that the difference between good people and average people was that good people appreciate what they have *before* they lose it, while average people only appreciate what they have after they lose it.

Using the EAT principles and anecdotes I've shared here, I outlined ways for those employees to put the company's problems into perspective and make their decisions based on the big picture.

If they were expecting me to give them a big hug and sympathize with their plight, they were certainly surprised. I challenged every single one of them, saying, "If you walk out because of this, you'll look back and wish you hadn't. Why? Because you've invested fifteen years of your life in this place."

They couldn't believe what I was saying—that I had the nerve to tell them to stick it out.

"The missing retirement funds amounts to a major mistake and I can't put the money back in your account," I said. "That one mistake takes away fifteen years and the memories and experiences that you love. But aside from the big mistake of destroying your retirement fund, is there anything else you hate about this company? If there is, raise your hand."

Not one person raised a hand.

I kept going. "You are being tested and I hope you think about what you're walking away from before you make your final choice."

I told them they had the resources and the leverage to have their concerns resolved in the company, but it was up to them to stay together as a group to get the company on the road to recovery. When I left, I left a group of people united to bring that company to a new level. They committed to keeping the right focus—on what they had in front of them, not what they saw on the other side of the fence.

Those people could have walked out the door of that company, complaining the whole time about the missing 401(k) money. And in the smaller picture, they would have been justified. But when they got to the next job, would they have been happier? They knew the answer was no. The answer for them was to dig in and fix the problems at the place they loved and rebuild it to where it had been. It's no different than a husband and wife who go through a rough patch, but realize that all the things that brought them together in the first place are still there. They're thankful they still have a chance to make things right.

Ironically enough (considering everything I've been saying about *why* versus *how*), there are a few how things you can do to open yourself up to a more thankful attitude. Start by taking time in your week to develop your attitude of gratitude. I do it by handwriting at least two thank-you notes every week. They don't have to be long or elaborate. Just a simple note with words of thanks for a gift or a gesture—or just because you appreciate who the recipient is in your life. Writing the note, putting it into an envelope, and mailing it (no e-mail, please) takes less than five minutes, and you'll be amazed at how good you'll feel after you do it.

If you can harness that positive attitude—and, most importantly, remember it when things might not be going as well—you'll notice a peculiar thing. What you choose to look for in life, you'll find. What you find, you'll attract. And what you attract, you'll become. That's the definition of destiny.

Some people are negative by nature, and they run from place to place looking for something external to make them happy. Why? Because it's easier. It's easier to ditch and run when something gets challenging. And it's why those people are ultimately disappointed at each stop and never satisfied.

I gave a talk to a small group once, and afterward, a man came up to me and said, "Bryan, I don't like where I am working any more and I've been here for fifteen years. I'm in sales and I'm really not doing well and I'm not very happy. Do you think I should change jobs?"

He had this nervous, hopeful look on his face, and I knew he was just dying for me to tell him it was okay to change jobs and find something that made him "happy."

"You shouldn't change jobs right now," I said, and his jaw almost hit the floor.

"If you change at this point, then you leave as a loser. You march through an imaginary door with a sign over the top that says, 'Loser,'" I said. "Today, make a decision to return to your company and fall back in love with your job like when you first started to work there. Raise your sales numbers until everyone wonders what in the world got into you, and you will become the hero of your environment. When you reach that top level, if you want to make a job change, then change."

He said, "Why do I need to wait until I reach the top?"

"Because if you leave when you are on top, you go through a different door. Anyone can go through that 'Loser' door. Let's see how well you can choose to change when you are on top, because it is the difference between being good or just average."

By working on the self-improvement plan in these chapters, you're choosing not to be average. You're accepting the idea that The Good Life doesn't come by delegating the responsibility for it to somebody else. That means you're going to have to work, but when you see the benefits, you'll know they're all yours.

Forty-Eight-Hour Action Plan

1. Make your own why lists: one for home, and one for work. Kate's story is at the top of my why list for work. Pick the most powerful inspirations, and limit them to three for each list.

2. Live the "on its time" rule strictly for the next two days. When you're confronted with a situation that needs resolution—a problem at work, an argument with a spouse or child—commit to addressing it and resolving it as quickly as possible.

3. Engage in a healthy debate about something that's been nagging at you. If you aren't used to dealing with confrontation, it will be uncomfortable. But the only way to develop the thick skin you're going to need for it is to start small. It can even be something as simple as telling your spouse you don't like it when he or she leaves the toothpaste tube out on the counter. As you work your way up to the bigger debates, e-mail me at thegoodliferules@bryandodge.com and tell me your story. If it's a good one, I'll interview you about it on my radio show, so you can inspire other people.

4. Write down the name, address, e-mail, and phone number of one person you haven't kept in contact with the way you would like. Put that note on your refrigerator door or bathroom mirror to remind you of what you need to do. Nervous? Don't worry, I'm going to help you through it in the next chapter.

Rule

4

Diminishing Intent, or Follow Your Heart in Forty-Eight Hours

You're going through your regular daily routine—driving in traffic, talking on the phone to a customer, sorting through the mail—when a thought pops into your head.

It could be the face of a person you haven't thought about for a long time. The final piece of a puzzle you've been trying to solve for months at work. An idea for the perfect gift for an important person in your life. The painful twinge of a mistake you've made that you haven't resolved with the person who was hurt. That phone call you haven't made yet. Or even the thought of someone close to you who is struggling with a serious problem—money, alcohol, drugs—and how you don't know what to do to help.

It's happened to all of us, but what is it? It's your brain—and your heart—trying to help you. Your subconscious mind and conscience are reminding you about the things close to your heart, or about important issues you might have forgotten. And once you get that flash of a thought in your head, it's your job to act on it before it falls beneath the surface again. Or before somebody else gets in your way and keeps you from acting on it in time.

That's what "diminishing intent" is. It's the distractions of the world ganging up to sidetrack you from resolving the important issues your brain and your conscience are trying to remind you about. Think about it like the in-box in your head. Somebody could bring by a really important contract for you to read over, in an envelope with a bright orange sticky note on the front. When that envelope is on the top of the pile, it's easy to see, and it's there reminding you that you need to take action. But if you ignore it, it gets buried by less important envelopes and wastepaper.

I don't have to tell you that life is the same way. We've all got cell phones ringing and e-mail messages waiting for our attention, and schedules and to-do lists and daily hassles hanging over us. Last week, I took three separate day trips—to Wisconsin, to Virginia, and to Florida. I also went to two soccer games, gave two presentations here in Dallas, and spent twenty hours of my time working on this book and another ten preparing for the *Building a Better You* radio show I do every Saturday on Dallas's WBAP. And I'm no different from most people. When the responsibilities of everyday life start to pile up, it's so easy for *all* of us to get paralyzed by fear, laziness, greed, or the conflicting agendas of the people around us.

We're going to get to some strategies for streamlining your life in Chapter 8, but first, I have to warn you about one of the unfortunate truths that come with the crowded lives we lead.

When you let yourself get distracted by the "small" things, you set yourself up to miss the big things. You set yourself up for regret. And the more regret you have, the less you're able to live The Good Life. I told you a little bit about Kate in the last chapter. When you hear the full story, you'll understand what I mean about acting on the things that matter—the things that touch your heart—before you lose your chance. Before you regret it.

Your head and your heart know those are the big things. It's time to listen.

Kate's Story

Kate was the daughter of the woman who for many years booked my flights. Kate was a normal, happy girl, with no medical problems of any kind that they were aware of. So Kate's mom worried about her when she came home one day and said she was short of breath and her head hurt. They went to the doctor, and he gave her some antibiotics for the throat infection and sent her home.

That night, Kate woke up in a sweat, and came into her parents' bedroom. "I just want you to know something," she said to them. "I love you more than anything in the world. I couldn't have asked for better parents. I just wanted to tell you that. I have this terrible feeling that I'm dying."

Kate had a virus that had attached to her heart and shrunk it. She would have needed a heart transplant to live if they had known earlier. She didn't live through that night.

In the course of a day, Kate's parents had gone from having a happy, carefree daughter to planning a funeral.

At that service, you couldn't fit another person in the church. I squeezed into a seat in the back, and before the funeral started, one of Kate's teachers came over to where I was sitting. She asked if she could share a story about Kate with me. At first, I didn't know why she would want to tell me. I wasn't a part of Kate's family. But in time, I realized she wanted me to use my platform as a speaker to share this story so it could help other people. As I mentioned briefly in the last chapter, Kate's story is one of the big "whys" in my life. It's why I get on planes when I'm tired of flying, and why I'm willing to spend time on the road when I'd rather be home with my family. It's one of those things that gets you up when you don't want to be up. It's inspiration that drives me when the days aren't so easy.

"Kate was my favorite student—so passionate about learning, and so open," the teacher said. "Every class I teach, I'm looking for another Kate, but she was one of a kind."

The woman touched the necklace around her neck, tears rolling down her face. "Kate gave me this. My dad loved it so much that Kate gave him one, too. That's just the way she was—so generous. A couple of weeks ago, Kate's name came into my head. I was looking forward to talking to her about how things were going in her life and what college she had decided to attend, and I wanted to thank her again for being such an inspiration. I meant to call her, and I only live a few blocks from her. But I didn't get to it. I let my life and my job run me, instead of the other way around. I figured there'd be plenty of time for us to catch up. Now, it's too late. Don't make the same mistake with the people you love."

Now, the next thought that comes to you out of the blue might not be such a life-or-death situation. But Kate's teacher didn't think hers was, either. So whether your thought is for a person you might lose or simply a conversation with a friend you need to have, committing to take action is so important.

How do you keep that commitment? By giving yourself a finish line with the forty-eight-hour key.

Forty-Eight-Hour Resolutions

Picture one of these spontaneous thoughts that come to mind as if it were a candle in your head being lit. At first the flame is tall and strong, but as you put off acting on that thought—resolving it in some way—the energy that comes with the thought starts to disperse. When a candle burns down to its bottom, the flame gets fainter and fainter.

The Good Life has two major components: recognizing the important things in your life, and acting on those things when you do identify them. Each of the chapters in this book will help you get better at identifying the things that are important to you. This chapter will help you stop being paralyzed and start acting on those things—before diminishing intent sets in. This is where the Forty-Eight-Hour Rule comes in.

As great as it feels to be able to see some of the important ideas that come into your head for what they are—life-changing opportunities—that's only one part of the puzzle. You've got to do something about them. And to me, a forty-eight-hour time period is the perfect framework for taking action, because it gives you time to prepare yourself—but not enough time to procrastinate. It's why I end all of the chapters in this book with forty-eight-hour action plans.

It's pretty easy to sit in the comfortable chair in your living room and say to yourself, "I'm going to walk into the office tomorrow and tell my boss I'd like a different assignment. I'm tired of not being challenged in my work." Or, "Tonight, I'm going to call my brother and work out this stupid disagreement we've been having for the last month."

I can tell you from firsthand experience, conviction and momentum are powerful things. In almost every talk I give, there's a part of the presentation where the energy in the room builds like it does at a college basketball game. I'm not talking about a superficial kind of excitement, like you'd hear from a motivational speaker—I've told you before how I feel about "motivation." I'm talking about genuine, heartfelt excitement. The people in the crowd are really animated—answering back as I say things and even cheering, and it doesn't matter if they're accountants, sales-people, or sports coaches.

When the energy is at its peak like that, it's easy for people to make big promises to themselves about taking action. My goal in those presentations—and here with you—is to give you the tools not just to make those promises to yourself but also to live up to them, before day-to-day life sucks the energy and inspiration from you.

I want you to take the next step.

By attaching a forty-eight-hour requirement to act on the thoughts that come into your head this way, you're essentially adding a "grade" to your performance. You can't say to yourself, I'll deal with it some other time. You can't just bury your thoughts again. Once you start to take action on these things, you'll find it's like emptying a lot of extra paper out of your mental filing cabinet. You're stripping away layers of stress and worry, and creating a new set of habits going forward.

I'll be the first to admit that these habits are ones you're always going to have to work on, because avoiding a decision—whether it's about something painful like a fight with a friend or relatively simple, like figuring out how to pay for new tile in the bathroom—is just easier in the short term. I still work on myself all the time.

Tying Up Loose Ends

A few years ago, I was spending a rare free Saturday afternoon out in my barn, with my horse, when a name I hadn't thought about in a long time popped into my head: Charles.

Charles was an acquaintance of mine who had been looking for a business partner four years before. We got to talking at a confer-ence, and I told him about another acquaintance who might have been a good match for his project. I also gave Charles the same advice I'd give my own kids—to make sure he did his research on the deal before he committed to it.

You can probably guess what happened next.

Charles plunged into a deal the next week and immediately lost $6,000 in goodwill money he had fronted to the other partner. When I heard about it, I felt very bad for Charles and, honestly, more than a little embarrassed about the part I had played in bringing them together. To his credit, Charles never blamed me for what happened. He was very up-front about the fact that he had jumped in too fast.

Here it was, four years later, and I couldn't get Charles's name out of my head. The next thing on my mind was, "I should send him some money to cover part of his loss on that deal." This was all happening around Christmas, so it seemed like something to do in the spirit of the season.

Of course, I had second thoughts about it. I don't care who you are—$3,000 is a lot of money to send off in the mail to somebody you haven't seen in four years and who didn't ask for it. Besides, I had been saving some money for a four-wheeler I wanted to buy to go out and ride around with my kids.

I went in the house and got ready for bed. When I tried to fall asleep, I tossed and turned for twenty minutes, until finally Margaret said, "Bryan, whatever you need to do, get up and do it. You are driving me nuts."

I said, "Before I do, I need to talk to you about this one."

She turned away from me. "It's late, and I'm exhausted. We're not talking about anything right now."

"Well, it's about $3,000," I said.

She sat up and switched the light on. We talked for more than an hour that night. I told her my thoughts and my doubts and how the idea of sending Charles $3,000 had come into my mind.

"Do it," she said.

"Wait a minute. That's easy for you to say," I said. "You haven't been saving the $3,000."

"When a call comes to your heart, you don't delegate it," she said. "You need to be the one that gets it done."

That night I typed up a letter to Charles:

> Dear Charles,
>
> I haven't heard from you in four years. I don't know why, but I want to send you a check for $3,000, half of what you lost on that referral. I appreciated that you never held it against me or my family.
>
> Sincerely,
>
> Bryan

Then I wrote the check, stuffed the letter and check into an overnight envelope, and sent it off.

Why did I immediately type the letter and write the check in the middle of the night? I'll be honest. If I hadn't done it immediately, I would have found a reason not to do it by the next morning. And for the next few days, I was half hoping he'd get the check, call me to tell me it wasn't necessary, and rip it up.

Then, three days later, my phone rang. It was Charles.

"Bryan, how did you know?" he asked.

"How did I know what?"

"That my wife and I lost our jobs." The company they both worked for had gone out of business, and they hadn't even had a week's notice or any kind of severance check.

"Charles, I didn't know anything about it."

He said, "Then you need to know one thing. Sharon is really sick. With the money you sent, I can check her in for the tests she needs."

I don't have to tell you that there isn't enough money in the world to buy the feeling I had after that call. And if I had waited another day, or a week, or just put it out of my mind for another four years, Charles's life would have been completely different. His wife's might have ended in a tragedy.

I'm not trying to say that I was some kind of hero. I'm saying we have far more impact on the lives of the people around us than we realize. And if we decide to make that impact a positive one, we *all* can do some incredible things.

A year later, I told Charles's story in a seminar I was giving in Dallas. Afterward, a woman came up to me. She had been crying, and she was wiping her eyes with a tissue. "I heard you six months ago, and today I brought my friends because I wanted them to hear the message," she said.

"When I first met you, I was very unhappy and angry. I was the one who was yelling at everyone, and cutting people off on the road," she said. "But when I left your seminar, I committed to one thing. Whenever a heartfelt thought came to my mind, I would act on it within forty-eight hours. And you know something? I've never been happier in my life."

She told me a story about a woman in her office—somebody who didn't have many friends in the building. "I thought about how lonely she must be, so I decided to ask her out to lunch the next day," she said. "When we met for lunch, she started crying even before we were seated. She said, 'I needed to talk to somebody. How did you know?'" The woman's husband had been diagnosed with cancer, and it was tearing their relationship apart.

They didn't know who to tell about it, or even how to talk about it with each other. A friendly, neutral person showed up at just the right time to simply listen.

I think we're *designed* to help other people; I think it's why we're here. It's not for the money and the house and the cars and the toys. Committing to the idea of following your heart within forty-eight hours helps get you back to the way you *want* to be. To the way you were *meant* to be.

Follow Your Instincts

Every time I touch on this subject in a presentation, hands shoot up immediately. "But how do we know what's important?" "How do we know what our 'heart' wants?"

Those are good questions.

I think you need to give your instincts more credit. How long does it take you, after meeting someone, to make a gut-level assessment about whether you like that person or not? Not very long. Sure, your opinion might soften later, or even change, but most of the time, your radar is pretty good.

When something comes into your head in the middle of the night and actually wakes you up, you *know*. Hey, I'm not talking about waking up in a sweat because you think you forgot to turn off the oven (but, by all means, go check to make sure you did . . .). When you wake up, get up and think about the fact that you haven't talked to your sister in three months, your instincts are telling you something. It's your subconscious giving you a little hint about something your conscious brain needs to work out.

Listen.

And if you don't fully trust your own instincts, there are some good indicators around you to take advantage of, too. Maybe you've got a trusted friend, or a mentor at work, or a parent or grandparent who really knows you and your values.

Heck, you might even have a dog. Yes, a dog.

At our house, we have a squadron of Labrador retrievers—Lexi, Ranger, Bailey, and Griz. I learned a long time ago that dogs are excellent judges of character. Why? Because instinct is all they have. You and I might be able to fake our way through a situation to try to get something we want, but life is a lot more basic for a dog. He either likes something or he doesn't. There's no agenda there. So you probably ought to pay attention.

My daughter, Nicole, knows all about the "dog thing" at our house. When various young men would come by to pick her up for a date, I'd let them get a few steps out of the car before I let the dogs out of the house. These aren't killer attack dogs or anything, but they would certainly protect Nicole if they felt she needed it. If the dogs got along with the young man, it said something about him. Not everything, of course, but a clue.

One night, Nicole came downstairs and said she was going out on a date. A half hour later, a car pulled up the drive, and a young man got out. I let the dogs out into the yard, and as soon as he saw them, he jumped back into his car. The dogs surrounded his car and started barking furiously.

Nicole was totally embarrassed that her dorky dad would pull the dog trick, so she grabbed her purse and hit the door at a near run. "I'll be home at eleven," she said.

"Make it 9:30," I said. "And keep your cell phone close."

At 9:00, Nicole walked in the front door. On her way up the steps, she said, without even looking at me, "The dogs were right, Dad."

Instincts don't give you all the answers. But they can tell you when something is wrong and motivate you to be a little more cautious or pay closer attention.

Acting Sets Things in Motion

Making the decision to take action within forty-eight hours can certainly be nerve-wracking, especially when you aren't sure what the final outcome will be. And the first few times you do it, you're going to be nervous and tentative because it's such a new skill. But one important thing to remember is that all the decisions you make when you commit to the forty-eight-hour rule aren't going to be negative ones. A lot of the things popping into your head are going to be positive things—opportunities for you to do something that makes you feel good.

A couple of years ago, I called my mom a week before her birthday and asked her what was on her gift list.

The question had become a running joke, because she always answered the same way—"Nothing. I have enough of everything, and I don't have any room for anything else. Just being able to talk to you is fine."

Now, it's one thing for your mom to tell you she doesn't want a gift. But you can't really just skip giving her a present, right?

For the past few years, I had spent time looking for the perfect card, and I inscribed it with a message and mailed it to her. When I hung up the phone with her this time, it came to me that I had to do something different for this birthday. I really wanted her to have something special this time.

Knowing she didn't want any "stuff," I started thinking about experiences I could set up for her, so she could enjoy her birthday in a special way.

I called my dad and asked which restaurant was Mom's favorite. "The Swiss Chalet in Woodland Park," my dad said, immediately. A friend of our family, Neil Levy, owned it, and my parents had been going there for years. I called the restaurant, and Neil was there. I told him I wanted to make a brunch reservation for two, for my mom's birthday. Neil said, "I've known your parents for over twenty-eight years and would be honored to take care of your mom on her birthday. This will make a really nice present."

I kept going. "Can we put something special on the table like some fresh flowers?" I asked.

"I'll be glad to handle that for you," Neil said. "What type of flowers?"

"Let's go with roses," I said.

"What color are you thinking? Yellow roses are beautiful."

Red would have been my pick, but I figured Neil was more of an expert on those kinds of things than I was.

On the big day, my dad brought Mom into the dining room at the restaurant, and everything was just perfect. The hostess greeted her at the door, wished her a happy birthday, and brought her to a special table with a fantastic view. It was decked out with a giant bouquet of yellow roses.

"Those are the most beautiful flowers I've ever seen," Mom said.

My parents were finishing up an amazing meal when they noticed an elderly couple at the next table.

"Look at the gorgeous flowers she has at her table," the woman said. The flowers on her table were smaller and slightly wilted.

When the waiter came to their table, the woman asked him about the difference in the two bouquets. He told her about the birthday celebration.

My mom leaned over to my dad and said, "I want to give half my flowers to her." My dad immediately jumped up, pulled half the roses from the vase, and went over to the next table.

"My wife would like you to have these flowers," he said.

The woman lit up, and said, "It's our sixtieth anniversary today. Thank you so much."

The man at the table looked a little embarrassed, but said, softly, "Yellow roses are her favorite. I wanted to get them for her, but finances are tight. I couldn't afford both the dinner and the flowers. Thank you so much for the wonderful gift."

My mom called me later to tell me the story. "You gave me a great birthday surprise, but the smile on that woman's face is what I'll remember about today," she said.

The decision to do something different and special for my mom set off a chain reaction of positive things. For me. For her. And for a complete stranger.

You've heard me say over and over again through these first four chapters that you need to find the important things in life. I really believe that's true. You learn to handle the distractions in your life better so you can spend less time on those and more on the things you love.

Still, every time I speak I get dozens of questions about how to determine what the important things are. You have to find them for yourself, but I can tell you what they *aren't*. They're not "stuff." New cars and big houses and all the toys are great. It's certainly nice to have them, as long as you're not chasing them to the detriment of the rest of your life. You can have the most beautiful car in the world, but if you don't have any gas, it's worthless. It's a giant paperweight in front of your house.

The Forty-Eight-Hour Rule creates the energy you need for the people who need you. It's the gas that moves the car.

Forty-Eight-Hour Action Plan

1. Commit to acting on the next thing that comes into your head—from your heart. Excuses are easy to come up with. Don't fall into that trap. And don't get intimidated if the thing that comes to you is big and complicated. You don't have to have it completely resolved in forty-eight hours. You just need to take action and get on the road to resolving it.

2. Slow down. When the thought comes to you, take the time to recognize it for what it is. Turn off the television, cell phone, and Blackberry and give yourself a chance to digest it. Just by taking this step, you'll become so much better at understanding the relative importance of things. In other words, you get better at editing out the noise.

3. Write it down. Putting your action statement on paper is a way of showing true commitment to it. It makes it real. A goal is only a wish until you write it down, and then it becomes a reality.

4. Pick a finish line. Within the forty-eight-hour time frame, pick an event that signals the deadline for your action plan. If there's a phone call you need to make, for example, tell yourself that by the time you get out of your car at the end of the day tomorrow, the call will be made.

5. Celebrate. Whether your action item is a positive or negative one, you're going to realize at the end of the forty-eight-hour period that you feel so much better being unburdened of something hanging over you. You need to celebrate the achievement, because The Good Life is about making these kinds of decisions consistently over your whole life. It's not about just doing it once. If you don't have some reward system in place, you're not going to stick with it over the long run. It's like a diet program. I don't believe in diets, because diets don't change the habits that caused the weight gain in the first place. Life change is what works. And you can do it.

Rule
5

Be Faithful

aithful is a word that elicits different reactions in different people. It might be a word that touches your heart immediately, and perhaps you're looking for some guidance about how to be more faithful. Or, you might be rolling your eyes, thinking you're going to get some standard Sunday school speech about how the important people in your life are counting on you, so you have to show up for them.

Either way, I think you'll be surprised about what I have to say about faithfulness.

We throw around terms like *faithful* all the time, but I believe that many people have a misconception that faithfulness has something to do with what *other* people or organizations do for them. In other words, people think that faithfulness is something you only offer when you expect something in return.

I disagree with that.

Sure, you would hope that the relationships you have are faithful ones—with your spouse, friends, or the company you work for. Everybody wants to have a relationship with somebody they can trust. But I believe faithfulness is something that you *are*, not a behavior or a strategy, and that being committed to somebody else—regardless of whether or not they're faithful to you—has value.

So many people feel they have to look out for themselves—and if that comes at the expense of other people, then so be it. The world is such a busy, connected place that it's tempting to go home and close yourself off from other people. It's definitely not like it was when I was growing up, when the world was only as big as the neighborhood you lived in, and your neighbors knew everything about you. Now, we have access to so much more—and, ironically, so much less.

In the United States, we're so lucky to have access to the best the world has to offer. If you want it, and you work for it, you can have the best of everything, right around the corner. I live outside of Dallas, and I don't have to go far to get the best steak, a world-class bottle of wine, or a $200,000 sports car. If I had the money, I could have them at my house in an hour. And if I drove to the Dallas–Fort Worth airport, I could fly anywhere I wanted to in the world. At no other time in the history of mankind have people had so many options.

But you could go see everything you ever wanted to see, eat the best of everything, and own everything you ever wanted to own, and you'd still feel an emptiness. I've talked to enough superrich people to know that it isn't the money that makes them happy. It helps, sure, but it isn't *the* thing. You can get everything you want, but to get what you *need*, you have to go out and work for it a little—and that's tough for some people. A lot of people never get it.

The bottom line is, when you can get outside yourself and do something for somebody else, that's what gives you ultimate satisfaction. And to be faithful, you have to get outside yourself—outside your own needs, wants, or even addictions. It's choosing to be faithful to a company, a team, a friendship, your marriage, or, as corny as it sounds, to your country.

Is it tough? Absolutely. We've all been the victims of broken promises. Companies have treated workers poorly. Spouses have been unfaithful. Friends haven't acted the way true friends would. The government has taken the trust given to it by the voters and betrayed it. But until you let that go, and learn to be faithful again, you won't be able to find the satisfaction that comes from giving and being connected to others.

Part of it comes from seeing more than just your own side of the story. That's certainly a challenge for all of us. Corporate leaders tell me that one of the main reasons they hire me to come and speak is so that I can help rebuild the trust on a team where it's been violated; they want me to come in and help people see the other side.

Seeing the other side creates chemistry, and chemistry is what lubricates your life for the long term.

I'll never forget my daughter's senior season on the high school soccer team. Just before the year started, the coach she'd spent her career with decided to resign to focus on being a full-time mom. My daughter loved her coach and was devastated when it happened.

The new coach came in, and she had some different ideas about playing time. My daughter went from being a starter to spending a lot of time on the bench. I told her that life wasn't fair, and that she had to keep her effort up and not quit. She understood right away, and she kept a great attitude and went on to play soccer in college. Fast-forward to four years later, and my youngest son was playing *his* senior soccer season. Three quarters of the way through the year, the coach had my son—who had started the whole year—start to split time with another player.

I remembered what had happened to my daughter, and I got ready to give my son the same talk, but he stopped me before I could even get the words out. "The other player needs more time on the field, or else he might quit the team," Zach said. "He's really tall, so we need him to help with headers when we have corner kicks."

Zach understood what it was like to be on both sides of the coin—something even I had needed to be reminded of. Just because the other player wasn't my son didn't mean he didn't have parents or friends who wanted to see him play, too.

We've been taught our entire lives that the side of the coin that lands faceup is the side that wins, and nothing else matters. But we confuse real life with a game. In real life, there's another side to that coin, and just because you can't see it doesn't mean it isn't there.

Anybody Can Do It . . . When It's Easy

It's easy to give everything you have to a person who is doing the same for you. Just like it's easy to agree to something your wife or husband asks you to do that you already love to do. "Honey, I need you to take this ice-cold beer and go over there and watch the football game," is not exactly a difficult request for a lot of people, right?

But it's what you do and how you act when things are tough that defines you as a person. If you can keep your head up—and your faithfulness intact—during the trying times, you're setting yourself up for a greater reward than the short-term satisfaction of telling off somebody who hurt you.

After I had been established in business for a few years, a guy started following me around, hounding me to give him a job doing outside sales. I brushed him off at first, but after a while I was impressed by his persistence.

Finally, I told him I'd take him on if he agreed to one condition: he would have to sign on for one year, working straight commission. I knew that if I didn't get that commitment from him, after a couple of months of struggling out of the gate—as every salesman does when he's learning the product—he'd give up. And that would be a waste of both his time and mine. I knew he had the talent and the work ethic; what I needed from him was the commitment. He agreed to the year, and we even put it in writing.

As predicted, he really struggled the first month. The second month was even worse; he made absolutely no money. The third month, he started to figure some things out, but he still wasn't making any money, and his wife was starting to come down on him about it.

By the ninth month, he was making more money than most people his age had ever seen. We became more than just business associates. We were friends. He worked his way up in my organization, all the way to vice president.

He and I spent months and hundreds of thousands of dollars putting together a marketing agreement to exclusively represent another prominent speaker on his tours. All of the pieces finally came together, and we were scheduled to sign all the papers on a Monday.

The Saturday before, the speaker called me to tell me how excited he was that the deal was signed.

"What?" I asked, knowing I hadn't signed anything yet.

He went on to say that my vice president and another man had brought the papers to him that day, and he was happy to sign on.

Later that day, I got a call from my vice president, who told me that he had made a deal with another company to deliver the project to them—in turn for half ownership of that company.

It was like somebody reached into my chest and ripped my heart out. I curled up on the couch in the corner of my office and cried. I felt so totally betrayed—that somebody I had put all that time and effort into did something so devastating to me, and to the sixty other employees at the company.

On Monday, when I went back to the office, I didn't go and tear up all the pictures on his desk or shove all of his stuff into boxes and leave it on the front step. I was just hurt. Very, very hurt.

Obviously, I fired my vice president that day. But a few weeks later, he called me. He gave me a heartfelt apology about the betrayal and told me that the man he had made the deal with had dumped him. He had nothing. He asked if there was any way he could have his job back.

I thought about it for a second, and I said he could come back.

Why? Because my heart called me to do it. He was a friend. He was more than a friend. He was family. There's no doubt things were different when he came back. The chemistry we had was gone, and the energy was different. It became just a job, and he was just an employee. And he sensed it too. A few months later, he came to me and thanked me for giving him another chance, but said he didn't think it was going to work out.

The best thing I ever did was let him come back. Not for him. For me.

It was a test of my faithfulness. Was I going to be a person who only was faithful when things were going my way? I could have slammed the phone down when he called asking to come back and lived the rest of my life with that hurt feeling. Too many people hold onto things like that for too long. They think that by doing it, it's going to hurt the other person and somehow "get them back." The sad part is, the other person forgets about it long before that. They just don't care.

That's why I let it go. I won't let somebody else break me—break who I am—which is a faithful, positive, honest person. I've made my share of mistakes, but my mistakes have never defined who I am.

Sometimes, people will try to use other people's mistakes to give themselves a sense of superiority. If you let negative people or bad business relationships make you cynical and suspicious, that means those people have won. They've beaten you.

Any businessperson would say I made a stupid decision. Dollars and cents say I did. But I'll live longer because of it, because I didn't have to carry that bitterness around. Money can't buy you more time.

I'm not trying to be crude, but life sucks at times. Life isn't fair. Go to a cancer clinic sometime, and you'll see people who should be angry at the world. But the most remarkable thing is that they aren't. Most of them have *total* faithfulness. They've let go of all the things that don't matter.

That's a lesson we all can learn. It's so important not to give up on yourself, even when you have those bleak times. And believe me, I know that the world isn't making it any easier for you to have faith in yourself.

We're all constantly being seduced by the easy life. If you want Indian food, you can get it delivered to your door. If you want to watch television—and the average American watches a ton of it, almost seven hours a day—you can switch to a hundred different channels. If something hurts, you can take a pill to make the pain go away. You can get anything you want.

But that's not where faithfulness comes from. The whole definition of faithfulness is that you're there when it's easy and when it's hard. The word doesn't mean much if you're only talking about the times when the credit card is empty and the refrigerator is full. Faithfulness is sticking to something when it's not easy.

Faithfulness gives you what you need. It produces the chemistry you have with the people who are important to you. But to get it, you have to go out and work for it a little.

Keeping the Faith, or Getting It Back

I can understand if you're discouraged by all this talk about a commitment to faithfulness being hard work. And I'm not going to sugarcoat it, it is work.

But you already have the skills to do it. And I can say that without even meeting you. How?

Because the secret to faithfulness is being you, consistently. It's showing up for the people who are important to you, even when it would be easier to take a day off. It's not some magic skill that takes an advanced degree. It's persistence. It's determination. It's understanding that the people who love you will understand your faithfulness by what you show them, not by what you say or promise.

I get up in front of thousands of people every week and talk about the same things I'm discussing with you right now. And I'd be the world's biggest hypocrite if I didn't live what I profess. I couldn't live with myself, and, more important, the people who know me would know I was a fraud. I'm not perfect by any stretch, but the thing I'm the most proud of is what I think my family would say about me if I weren't around. I think that's a pretty good goal for anybody to shoot for.

I make more than three hundred appearances around the country every year, but I do whatever I can to avoid staying overnight. If that means getting up at 4 A.M. to feed the horse and the dogs and catching the 7 A.M. flight out of Dallas so I can be back after dinner, then that's what I do, because I want to be home for my family.

A few years ago, I flew to Houston to speak to a group of 1,200 teachers and then caught a shuttle back that afternoon. As I was driving back to the house from the airport, I got a call from the local Fox affiliate. They were putting together a story about why some teenagers seem to get along great with their parents, and they wanted to come out and shoot at the house at dinnertime.

I said I'd have to check with the boss first, and I called Margaret. My son Zach answered the phone, and he said that Mom had gone to the movies.

I called the Fox people back and said that if they didn't need to shoot in the house—Margaret doesn't like those kinds of surprises—and they could get it done in an hour, I'd talk to them. I didn't want to waste too much time because it was a perfect afternoon, and Zach and I were going waterskiing.

When I got out of the car in front of our garage, Zach was getting the ski boat ready.

"I've got a surprise for you," I said, as the Fox satellite truck pulled in behind me.

"Did you do something wrong?" Zach asked, eyeing the truck and the cameramen who were getting out of it.

I hadn't thought of that, and I laughed.

Before I had a chance to say anything, the reporter walked over to Zach and put the microphone in front of him.

"Your dad flew back from a talk in Houston this afternoon so he could go waterskiing with you. I've known him for almost fifteen years, and he's always been that way. What does that tell you?" he asked.

Zach paused for a minute, and his lower lip started to quiver.

"It tells us he loves us," Zach said.

I gave him a hug and told him—with a laugh—that I'd forgive all the mistakes he had made in his life.

Our household isn't an easy one. We've had all kinds of adventures—and misadventures—happen to us over the last few years. In each of the last six years, we've had some major health scare—everything from blown out knees to a broken back to viral meningitis.

But the reason I have what I have is because I'm faithful. My kids and my wife know they can count on me, that I'm going to be there when things are great and when they are rotten. They know that I love them not because of what they give me or do for me, but because of who they are.

When I come home, my kids say, "Hi, Dad," because that's who I am. They don't say, "Hi, neighbor," "Hi, friend," or "Hi, Bryan." When you have a child and you see that baby for the first time, you know that feeling of unconditional love. Unfortunately, for some people that feeling fades, and being in a family becomes drudgery. But that initial feeling hasn't faded for me—I remember it every day.

I'm not trying to say I'm some superhero father or husband. I'm just a regular guy. I'm not supersmart, or super anything. I'm not doing anything anybody else couldn't do. But I'm committed to being faithful to my family. I'm blessed with a lot of energy, and I've committed myself to bringing that energy home.

My role models for bringing energy home are my parents. In the basement of their house they have dozens of boxes of reel-to-reel tape, footage they shot of my brother, my sister, and me growing up.

Lots of families have home movies. Those my parents shot showed just how faithful they were to us through a lot of hard times, and good ones, too. The movies showed us being us, amid the ups and downs of family life.

The idea of family that those tapes represent really hit home for me a few years ago, when I came up with a clever Christmas gift idea for my parents. I snuck into the basement and took the tapes to my house. I spent two days watching them all. I saw my brother's first diaper change and his graduation from college—and everything in between. I watched my sister grow up the same way and then watched myself. I called my brother and sister and asked them to tape what they'd tell Mom and Dad if they had only one last chance. Then, I worked with a video editing company to splice together highlights of each kid, with music and then the recorded messages at the end.

When we all got together at Christmas, I gave my parents a DVD of the video.

"This is something money can't buy," I said. "We just want you to know how much we appreciate the love you showed us, no matter what."

That DVD has become a tradition in my parents' house. My mom gets up in the morning on each of our birthdays and watches the clips from each child. She says it's like getting a brand-new present on *our* birthdays, just like when we were born.

You *do* have what it takes to be faithful. You just have to be you. Every day. Show the people you love they can count on you and you'll have everything you ever need.

You might be thinking that that's easy to say when things are going well. But it's true even when you're facing a loss—the death of a loved one, or some other less painful setback like the loss of a job or the breakup of a friendship.

One thing we're guaranteed in life is that we'll experience loss. People die. Things break. Life isn't fair. I'm not trying to be harsh, but those are the realities we face. The key is to learn how to lighten your load so you can move forward. Faithfulness is what connects you to people who can help you do that.

Find Your Priorities

It should be pretty obvious by now that a critical part of being faithful is choosing the priorities in your life. You can't do it all, and you can't be it all. If you try, it will just lead to frustration and disappointment.

As I write this, I can hear a report on television in the next room about some American families struggling with a mortgage that has reset to a higher interest rate, and they're in danger of losing their homes. That's an awful thing, and I don't want to minimize that pain.

But what are a lot of us chasing? Our world tells us that if we're driving a luxury car, or living in a big new house, we're living The Good Life—even if we've overdrawn our checking account and are sixty days from losing everything.

I believe that being faithful in how you handle your money is another way to be faithful to the people who are important to you. My company produced a software program, Debtwork.com, that analyzes your complete financial picture and gives you a red or green light depending on how well you're doing at eliminating your debt.

Can you imagine what would happen if each of us actually had that kind of light on top of our house? If every house in America had a light on it like that—showing green if you were being faithful in terms of your money, or red if you weren't—how do you think people's focus would change? I think we'd have a different set of status symbols, for sure. If you had a red light on your house, you'd be focused on turning it off, so your neighbors (or coworkers) wouldn't see it. You wouldn't go buy a new car and expect your buddy to come over and admire it in the driveway. You'd expect him to call you an idiot because you financed the whole thing with that red light glowing on top of the house.

Why is it that we'd do just about anything to avoid being embarrassed in front of people we don't know, but we're not faithful—financially or otherwise—to the people who actually live *in* the house with us?

I'm not saying that all material possessions are bad, or that you shouldn't have a big house or a nice car as a goal, or as the payoff for success in business. I've got a nice house with a nice barn behind it, and I've got a new truck and a sweet ski boat. I love my toys, and my life would be less fun if I didn't have them. But a big house and a fancy car and a ski boat, although nice accessories, shouldn't be your main reason for being here.

In the United States, we can choose so many things, from our food to our relationships and our jobs. We can choose wisely or poorly. But the faithful part isn't optional. Being faithful is being true to the people around you, and true to yourself. It's what you're here for.

It comes down to deciding that you want to listen and know people—to show people that you're in a listening mode, not a telling mode. If the only thing you take from this chapter is the idea that you can decide to be faithful and to want to know people—instead of being so self-interest driven—I've been successful. To live The Good Life Rules, you're not choosing to be somebody, you're choosing to *know* somebody. A lot of people have acquaintances. The Good Life is having friends—before you need them.

Know When to Let It Go

The most painful conversations I have are with the people whose hearts have been almost permanently broken by someone important in their lives. It could be a wife whose husband has cheated. It could be a friend who has repeatedly had his trust betrayed.

These people are in so much pain, and they ask me how I can talk about the willingness to be faithful to others who have done so much damage.

As optimistic as I am about human nature, I know there are some people who just can't be faithful. They don't have it in them to do what comes so naturally to most of us, to build strong, trusting relationships with people we love and who love us.

I believe it's your job to be a faithful person. But if you can't get through to a person in your life— if you can't change the person's bad behavior—then you have to *change the person*. In other words, when you've lost the hope that you can get to them, it's time to let them go.

If someone is abusing you physically, emotionally, sexually, or even financially, you don't owe faithfulness to that person. You owe faithfulness to yourself and your own safety. What's important is that you don't lose the *ability* to be faithful. You had faith in the beginning. You married the person. You tried to help him or her. You tried to be a friend. You tried to work with that person. You can't let the horrible experiences contaminate your ability to offer faithfulness again. You might have lost your ability to be faithful because somebody took it from you, but this is your time to get it back.

Today is about today, not about yesterday. If you get back to being faithful, you're getting back to something money can't buy. It's one of the most valuable things you can offer to another person. Do you know how many wealthy people I talk to month after month who are near tears because they feel that life is so empty? They tell me they'd give millions back if they could just have somebody in their life—a friend, a spouse—who they knew was there for them. That tells you how important money is in the grand scheme of things. It's nice to have, but you'd certainly rather have the faithfulness.

Back when I was traveling around the country and developing programs for other speakers, I decided that I wanted to enter a new market in the Midwest. I took my son John aside and told him that I'd be gone for almost nine weeks, and that I needed him to help his mother out around the house, feeding the horses and taking care of the dogs.

"I have my own goals on my trip," I told him. "If you hit your goals when I'm gone, what would you like for a reward?"

He answered almost before I could finish.

"A bike."

We hopped in the truck and went into town, where he pointed out the bike he had picked out. He got on it, and I took a picture of him.

I made a deal with John. If I went on my trip and hit my goals, and he held up his end of the bargain at home, when I got back, we'd get the bike.

Fast-forward six weeks.

It was the worst six weeks of my career. Nothing went right, and everything I touched just turned to rust. I had really lost complete faith in my ability to work in this business. I went back to my hotel room and called Margaret to tell her I was coming home. The call went through, and it was Johnathan who answered.

"Dad, I've met all my goals," he said. "Do you think I'll get the bike?"

That was just about the lowest I've ever felt. I knew that if I told my son that I had quit, he'd learn that quitting was something that was acceptable in life. I knew that John and Margaret had faith in my ability to provide for them. I needed to have that same faith in my own abilities and work harder to try to make the trip a successful one.

"Tell your mom I'll call her tomorrow with an update," I said, and hung up the phone.

The next day turned out to be a good one. I salvaged the trip, and yes, John did get his new bike.

I know I'm so very fortunate to have people in my life who have been with me through both the tough times and the great ones. Even if you don't have somebody like that in your life right now—a spouse, a friend, a relative—don't give up hope. Someone—and it could be a total stranger—will show you that keeping your faith in the idea of commitment wasn't a waste.

Forty-Eight-Hour Action Plan

1. Don't say you're committed; show it. It's easy to promise your child that you'll be at the soccer game on Monday. Don't promise. Go. Instead of pledging to your boss that you'll grow the business, do it.

2. Apologize. Pick a person important to you who deserves a "sorry," and make that happen. We've all been unfaithful to a degree—it could be a little white lie, a bill that wasn't paid on time, or phone call that wasn't returned. Take this forty-eight hours to make something right.

3. Make two lists. One, a list of things to which you've been committed, and another, a list of things to which you haven't been as faithful. The items on the lists can pertain to your financial life (balancing the checkbook, contributing to your 401(k) plan, getting out of debt [visit Debtwork.com]), your physical well-being (exercising regularly), your work-home balance (spending time with your family), or anything else that you think is important. This isn't necessarily about "sins." It's about committing to running your life better.

4. Only promise what you can deliver. You'll stop promising so much, and your life will be much better because of it. When you overpromise, you have to carry that with you when you can't deliver, and it weighs on you. That regret is bad for you, and it keeps you from having The Good Life.

5. Spend time with people who are faithful. Write down the names of three people who are the type of solid friends you'd like to be. Make them a priority when it comes to your time each week.

Rule

6

Create New Habits

We've spent the last five chapters talking about The Good Life Rules that you need to reconnect with the *why*. And I believe getting the why in life is the most important thing any of us can do.

In this chapter, though, we're going to take a short break from the why and touch on some of the *how*.

You've made a commitment to learn and to change. You understand why you follow your heart within forty-eight hours of being called to do something. And you know why being faithful to yourself—and to the people who are important to you—is so critical.

All of those things are big, big steps.

As much as I'd love to be able to promise that you could snap your fingers and have everything you want and need, the reality is different.

We all have a set of habits we've fallen into over the years. Many of those habits are great: When dinner is done, you automatically get up to help with the dishes, or when the Girl Scouts come to your door selling cookies, you're automatically generous. Maybe you're great about taking care of your body, and you work out regularly. Or you're the person in your group of high school friends who does the best job staying in touch (I call that person the "glue," and for us, it's Brian Werner).

On the other hand, we all have habits we aren't as proud of. Maybe you're not good with money or you smoke a pack of cigarettes a day. You might eat too much sugar or have an addiction to caffeine.

Your beliefs are one thing, but your habits are the sum total of what you are as a person, day to day. Show me your habits—and the people you spend your time with—and I'll show you where you are in life.

The point here is not for me to make a judgment about your habits. I just want to put *you* in a position to make an honest assessment of them. I want you to make a conscious decision to pick the habits you're going to have. Once you do that, you take control of your life, instead of letting your habits control you. And that's certainly one of The Good Life Rules.

Good and Bad Habits Come from the Same Place

If you think I'm getting ready to tell you about all the things you're going to have to stop doing because they're bad for you, you're 100 percent wrong. Certain habits are bad for you physically (like smoking or eating too much) and financially (charging more than you can afford on a credit card). But like I said before, my goal in this chapter is to get you to see what you're doing day in, day out and to make conscious decisions about whether or not to continue. Don't just fall into a mindless rut of habits.

Human nature is very, very basic. We're all driven by pleasure. We like to do things that make us feel good—even if the long-term impact of that behavior is negative. Cigarettes are a great example. Nicotine is a drug, and when you inhale it in a cigarette, it makes you feel good. I know, because I chewed tobacco for a long time. You become addicted to the sensation the nicotine gives you. Alcohol and food do the same, for the person who is addicted to the sensation.

The other powerful piece of that addiction puzzle is the social component. You might know smoking or eating too much is bad for you, but it's something you do when you're around friends. You don't want to give up the social aspect of the habit, and you rationalize the physical risks. But the same drive that sends people out to the front of the building to smoke in twenty-degree weather is what pushes people to get up at six in the morning and work out. The workout people are just getting that high in a different way.

Obviously, not every habit has a physical component to it. When you're talking about things in the "responsibility" category, like managing money or organizing your time, habits are tied to knowledge and resistance.

Knowledge is a pretty obvious element: you might be managing your money poorly because nobody showed you how to do it properly. I struggled with that for a lot of years because my parents believed that money wasn't something family should talk about, and so I didn't learn how to manage it.

The other piece is resistance, as in the path of least resistance. You might have fallen into the habit of eating some less-than-healthful foods because it's easier to stop at the drive-through on the way home than it is to figure out what kind of healthful meal to make at home. Or you might be paying a lot of interest on your credit card or your mortgage because you haven't taken the time to investigate better alternatives.

There's no doubt people are drawn toward inertia. If you're not pushed to do something for your immediate comfort, it's awfully easy to put it off until it becomes a bigger problem. Add in the fact that so much of modern life is about convenience—making things faster, cheaper, and easier—and it's easy to see how we get caught in that trap.

The companies that sell bottled water can talk all they want about how people buy it because of how pure it is, but I believe the real reason it sells is because you can carry it with you. My kids were drinking a lot of Coca-Cola—mostly because it's what was in the refrigerator. I didn't like that they were drinking so much sugar and caffeine, so I went and bought a pallet of bottled water from Sam's Club. My neighbors must have thought I was getting ready for the end of the world. But I just stuck the bottles of water in the refrigerator instead of Coke, and once the water became convenient, the kids grabbed it and didn't miss the soda.

What I'm trying to get you to see here is not some big laundry list of bad habits to fix. I want to show you that untangling all these habits and picking the ones you want to have isn't a giant wall to climb.

The basic truth about habits is that they're something you simply repeat, time after time. If you can decide to focus on a habit you want to have, and decide to do it for twenty-one days, you'll train your brain, and body, to think of what you've *picked* as the path of least resistance. You'll be working with your physiology, and not against it.

Define What's Good and Bad—for You

Let me say again that I'm not some Puritan who thinks you shouldn't enjoy yourself over a beer or cigar. That's really not the point of what I'm saying here; I want you to define your habits yourself.

The habits that control you, rather than vice versa—the ones you can't easily get away from—are the bad ones. I could tell you a dozen stories about drug or alcohol addiction here, but I think you already know that those are habits to get away from. It's the subtle habits that can sneak up on you.

When my company got up and running at full speed, my family and I decided we wanted to fulfill a long-term dream and move to a house on a lake. We found the perfect spot, in Lucas, Texas. I could hook my boat up to the truck and be on the water five minutes after leaving my driveway. However for the first six years we lived in Lucas, I don't think I made it to the lake more than six times, total. My office was on a direct line between the airport and the house, and I'd make it a habit to stop and check just one more thing at the office when I was coming home from a trip.

That "one more thing" usually became two or three more things, and I routinely rolled in at seven or eight at night. Working too hard—or too inefficiently—is definitely a bad habit. I finally got the message from my wife, who asked me one night why we even bothered to move to the lake, since we never saw it. So I moved my office so that it was in the opposite direction of the airport. We saved up some money and bought a Nautique ski boat, and I committed myself to be home in the afternoons, when my kids got back from school, so we could go waterskiing. Now, in the summer, we're out on the lake six days a week.

To assess your own habits, you've got to be honest with yourself. You might have something you've been doing in your day-to-day life that was "okay" to do for a long time, because you were younger, stronger, or more focused. How you eat is a great example. Your metabolism changes as you get older, and just because you consider yourself a healthy eater—for a thirty-five-year-old—doesn't mean you're going to be a healthy fifty-year-old. If you don't monitor your habits, those sandwiches you eat for lunch when you're thirty and fit could turn you into a chubby middle-aged guy.

By taking care not to let your habits control you, you're going to be able to do a better job keeping your life in balance and proportion. It's not about chopping all the things you enjoy out of your life and following some grim no-fun plan. I like wasting time as much as anybody. I've just figured out a mix of habits that works for me.

Let me use alcohol as an example. I've got some serious alcoholism in my family, and I know that being a hard drinker is something that would get me in trouble pretty fast. But I don't believe making a rule that I won't ever be able to go to Germany and enjoy a beer at Oktoberfest, or taste a fantastic wine from a friend's cellar is the solution. I could be a regular drinker and get to the point where I was going to have to take the drastic step of cutting all alcohol from my life—like some of my friends have had to do. Or, I could be honest with myself about my limitations and set a system in place that would allow me to enjoy myself in moderation. I decided to eliminate hard liquor from my life and restricted my drinking to nonschool nights—Friday and Saturday.

The key to The Good Life is to stay in control of your habits so they don't control you—and force you to do something drastic later. People develop diabetes in their middle-age years partially because they couldn't control themselves with food. Would you rather pass up an extra slice of pie now and then or stop eating it forever when you're fifty-five? To me, it's an easy choice.

But the truth is, the things that make it so easy for us to live in America make it easy to keep a hold of whatever habits we have, too. No society in the history of the world has had as much access to food as we do right now. Grocery stores are bursting with every kind of food you can imagine—and even some our parents couldn't have imagined, thanks to food science. And while it's great that frozen food can remain edible for months and your kids can enjoy green ketchup if that's what they really want, millions of people in this country are obese because their idea of a meal is something you pick up at a fast-food restaurant.

The second part of that equation is the fact that we just don't need to expend as much energy to live as we used to. Much of our lives are spent in cars, planes, and elevators. A lot of people aren't even doing something as simple as walking behind a lawn mower anymore.

Those might be explanations for what's happening to many people today, but I don't think they're excuses—any legitimate ones, anyway. As I said, The Good Life is about gaining control over the things in your life you *can* control, and habits are some of those things.

Do you want to change your bad habits? Do you wish you could quit doing some of the things that are wasting your time, hurting your health, or otherwise getting in the way of The Good Life? It doesn't matter if you're nodding your head yes to those questions because you're personally sick and tired of being sick and tired, or if you're motivated to kick your bad habits so you can be more active with your kids or more productive at work.

Regardless of what your motivation is, if you want to work on your habits, keep reading. I can show you some of the things that made that process less of a struggle for me.

Use Your Addictions Productively

Anybody who's ever tried to stop smoking or fingernail biting—or any other deeply ingrained habit—knows that human nature isn't something you just click off, like a light switch. We're all creatures of habit, and when we get into a pattern, it's not as simple as just changing the pattern, cold turkey.

Physiologically speaking, it takes at least twenty-one days for your body to start to let go of a habit or an addiction to something like caffeine, sugar, or nicotine. But it takes your mind a lifetime to get away from the triggers that make you want to drink a diet soda, eat some chocolate, or smoke a cigarette.

Why twenty-one days for your brain to adjust? Researchers have done all kinds of studies about addiction that point to three weeks or a month time frame, but for me, the most vivid representation of this was hearing about doctors during World War I having to amputate limbs under horrible conditions. The soldiers could feel pain in limbs that were no longer there, and it didn't start to fade until three weeks after the operations.

The first step is to beat the physical addiction component, by focusing and pushing through the first twenty-one days. The reverse is true as well, in terms of *starting* a habit. If you want to exercise regularly, you need to do it for twenty-one days—preferably in a row—to establish the "addiction" to working out.

The lifetime step is to get your mind focused on something besides the habit you want to get rid of. That's where habit replacement comes it. What you're doing is using your brain's desire to form a habit—or addiction—to your advantage. By deciding to replace your addiction with something else, you're helping your brain to refocus.

Have you ever met someone for the first time, and the moment your hand left his, you had already forgotten his name? It's because you weren't *there*. You weren't focusing on the task at hand. I meet upwards of fifty people a day, on average, and my business depends on remembering names and faces. I consciously slow down and focus on each one. I focus on what color eyes each person has. I recite the name again to myself, after I hear it, and I make a conscious decision to remember it. All of that comes before I even start listening to what the person has to say—and definitely before I start worrying about what to say back.

Rewiring yourself in terms of your habits works exactly the same way. Deciding to focus is the big step, and it's a powerful one. The question you're left with is, what do you replace the old habit with? Ask for guidance or think about something you've always wanted to try, like learning a new language or playing the drums, and go for it. Or, you can keep *parts* of the old rituals in place, but figure out a new, healthier format.

Let's say you love to eat. When your family gets together, you all eat and talk late into the night. It's a great scene, and the picture of emotional health and stability. But if everybody in the picture is forty pounds overweight, something has to change.

Is the answer to just cut all that out and not do it? Of course not. One family I know did the dinner part, but instead of sitting at the table for hours after, laughing, arguing—and eating more—they got up and walked.

Smoking is an extremely powerful addiction, both because of the nicotine and because of the rituals involved. You're asking too much of your body and your brain to simply stop, cold turkey, without replacing the smoking ritual with something else. People I know have had success with some of the nicotine replacement patches and gums you can buy, but I think it's important to do it without the "crutch" of medication, because you don't want to feel like you'll get dragged back into being a smoker if for some reason you don't have access to the gum or the patch.

It doesn't matter what you pick as a replacement habit—as long as it isn't harmful. It could be knitting (because it keeps the hands busy), or woodwork. Just pick something.

Don't let the habit pick you.

When I was ten years old, I was at a junior rodeo with a friend of mine, and we somehow found a can of chewing tobacco. If you know anything about rodeo, you know that chewing tobacco is almost as much a part of the sport as rope. We thought we were pretty sneaky. Until my dad caught us with it. Instead of beating my butt, he went and got another can of chew. He said, if you're going to try it, let's try it together.

You can probably guess what happened next. I took a giant hunk of tobacco out of the can and shoved it in my mouth. You're supposed to spit all the juice out. I didn't. It felt like an electrical current ran through my entire body, and I turned completely white. Then, I threw up, more and more violently, than I ever have since. That experience was enough to scare me off chewing tobacco. Until college.

I was back doing rodeo, and it was so much a part of the culture there that I started in with it again—taking care to spit all the juice out. Margaret hated it, and she constantly asked me to stop. I wouldn't—or I couldn't.

It wasn't until my daughter was born, and Margaret asked me if I wanted this baby girl to see me spitting tobacco juice, that I knew I had to change that habit.

I chewed enough gum to keep Wrigley in business forever, and I went and exercised every time the cravings got particularly bad. I put my running shoes on and ran (or walked) a few miles, or got on the treadmill. I'm not going to lie to you and say it was easy, but my brain slowly latched on to the endorphin rush that comes from working out as a replacement for the rush I got from the chew. It was so tough to do some of the things I had enjoyed so much with a chew in my mouth—like riding my horse, hunting, or just being out on the boat.

Like I've said before, I have an addictive personality, and it was very easy for me to get back into the habit of chewing. That's why it was so important to replace that addiction with something else. And having the motivation of a new daughter was a powerful part of that.

The Single Habit You Need for the Rest of Your Life

We've been talking about a menu of good and bad habits and how to identify the ones that work and the ones that don't work for you. I'm not here to judge you about what habits make up your life, but I do want to tell you about a habit that's been a constant for all the successful people I've ever dealt with: setting goals.

You're probably saying to yourself, "That's nothing new . . . I've heard that my whole life."

Maybe, but I'm not talking about things like "One day it'd be cool to have a snowmobile," or "I really should start working out again."

I'm talking about taking the time to come up with a set of short- and long-term goals and writing them out. I take it one step further and laminate my list—because when you laminate something, it can travel with you, and goals should always travel with you—and keep it with me in my wallet.

Why? Because of Lou Holtz.

I had booked the Hall-of-Fame former Notre Dame football coach for one of the seminars I had organized, and before the show we introduced ourselves and talked a little bit. After a few minutes, he asked me if I wanted to see his goals.

How do you say no to Lou Holtz?

He pulled a piece of paper out of the front pocket of his shirt and handed it to me. Before I had a chance to get to the first one, he said, "Now let me see yours."

I felt like he had set a fishhook in my mouth.

"I don't have them," I stammered. Here I am, running a company with more than sixty full-time employees, and I don't have my goals—even though I had heard plenty of times how important it was to set them, write them down, and carry them with you.

He pulled the paper from my hand, folded it, and put it back in his front pocket. "You can't see mine until you show me yours," he said.

I swore that day that I would never be in that position again. Not just in case Lou Holtz happened to stop by my house, but because I wanted to know just what it was I was shooting for.

I went home that night and wrote down my five goals:

1. Be a good husband.
2. Be a good father.
3. Read every day.
4. Work out four times a week.
5. Focus on why I'm doing what I'm doing, not only on how to do it.

I didn't stop there. I asked my wife and children to make their own lists, and then I took the three lists down to the Kinko's in town and had them all laminated. I gave a copy of them back to each person, and I carry a copy of all them with me.

We go through the ritual of setting new goals once all the ones on the list have been completed—not like temporary New Year's resolutions, but real, permanent life changes.

As my kids got closer to age sixteen, I told each of them that if they accomplished their list of eighteen goals, I'd give them a car for their birthday (as long as it cost less than $400—I'm not made of money). My daughter (the oldest) ripped through her list, and thirty days before her birthday, I bought her a white Ford Mustang. Why thirty days before? Because handing the keys to a newly minted sixteen-year-old and watching her tear out of the driveway in a new car would have been asking for trouble. Instead, she got the car when she couldn't drive it yet, and she had some time to get used to the fact that it was there.

When she did turn sixteen, and drove off for the first time, my next oldest, John, pulled on my sleeve. He had seen Nicole succeed—and that's really what this book is about, making goals and following through on them—and he wanted The Good Life for himself.

He handed me his list, and I made the same deal with him. When he turned sixteen, I took him to Colorado Springs and bought him my dad's used Ford F-150 truck (hey, boys drive crazier than girls . . . I know firsthand). He drove that truck until Zach turned sixteen, and then Zach took it over. The prize at reaching their goals kept each of them focused—on homework, staying in shape, not getting tattoos—and taught them very early in life what happens when you have something concrete to shoot for.

I'll never forget the day John came to me and said he was thinking about getting a tattoo. Now, I don't have anything against tattoos. I have something against inconsistency in enforcing the rules and following goals. John had put down on his goals list that he wasn't going to get a tattoo. And because he succeeded, he got a truck.

So I asked him if he really, really wanted a tattoo. Because if he did, he could give me the keys to his truck. I even told him I hoped he'd get some nice ink, because it would save me a lot of money in gas and insurance.

He thought about it for a second, then said, "No, I'll keep the truck." He didn't say I was mean. He didn't say I was out of touch. He understood that life is about choices, and that everything you do has consequences.

Lou Holtz didn't just change my life. He changed my entire family. I don't have enough pages in this book to tell you about all the great things that have happened to me and my family because we became focused on our goals. Why is this supposedly simple step so important?

Because picking goals isn't an option. It's a responsibility. If you don't take the time to do it, somebody else is going to do it for you. It might be your supervisor at work. It might be somebody else in your family. The point is, you will have lost control of the direction of your life. At the risk of sounding melodramatic, let me compare it to another worst-case scenario. If you have children, you don't get to decide not to feed them. If you do that, the state will come and take your kids away, and somebody else will feed them.

Goal setting is a nonnegotiable part of living by The Good Life Rules.

My family was sitting out back, in front of a big fire, laughing late into the night. As it got to be 1 A.M., it was just me and my daughter's boyfriend, Patrick, left.

It hit me that he was trying to figure out how to ask me The Big Question—for permission to marry my daughter.

Instead, he surprised me. "Can I show you what my goals are?" he asked, pulling out a piece of paper. "I'd like you to tell me if they're balanced and complete."

I scanned the list and told him they looked great to me.

"Good. Because when I hit these goals, I plan to come back and ask for Nicole's hand in marriage," he said.

Basically, he was having the meeting before the meeting, and I couldn't have been more impressed.

Months later, he called me and told me he'd completed his goals. I told him that we had to meet in person to talk about this, and since he lived in Austin and I was in Dallas, we met halfway, in Corsicana.

I had been thinking and thinking about what to say to Patrick, because I only had one daughter and one chance at this, and I wanted it to be right. I talked to my friends, who had been through it before, to try to get a sense of what I should do. I think I had twenty-one questions for Patrick, and I memorized them all so I wouldn't get nervous and forget them.

When we got out of our trucks to go and run my dogs and talk, all the questions I had memorized drifted away.

"I have one question for you," I said. "Do you know why my daughter picked you?"

He said yes.

"No, you don't," I said. "She picked you because she sees more in you than you see in yourself. Can you promise me that if my daughter gives her life to you, you'll give her everything she sees?"

His eyes got wide, and he leaned toward me. "How much does she see?" he asked.

"The mother lode."

For me, the saddest part of this chapter is that many people will appreciate that they need to make some changes in their habits, but they'll never do it. Life is full of distractions for all of us, and many people see goal setting as something "soft" that they can put off until they're less busy.

I've been talking about goal setting in my presentations for more than ten years, and I've heard tens of thousands of people promise me they'll go home and write a list of goals that same night. I even give out my e-mail address (goals@bryandodge.com) and ask them to send me a copy of the list. For every thousand people I speak to, I get a hundred goal lists.

The sad part is that most people miss the chance to really change their lives.

But the bright side is that the folks who do make a list and take the time to send it to me usually stay in touch. And I get the most wonderful follow-up e-mails weeks and months later about just how much the simple act of goal setting has changed lives.

So I challenge you to commit to writing down your goals and e-mailing them to me within forty-eight hours. Because the real truth is that if you don't do it in forty-eight hours, you'll get distracted, and you'll probably never do it.

If you do make the commitment and send your goals to me, at goals@bryandodge.com, I'll send you a special gift.

Forty-Eight-Hour Action Plan

1. Start by making a list with two columns—one for the things you're doing well in life, and the other for things you'd like to improve on. The goal isn't to make these a comprehensive catalog. Concentrate on the half dozen or so items that are really important to you.

2. Pick one thing from the "improve" list and resolve that you're going to stop it (or change it) within forty-eight hours. You're welcome to haggle with yourself about which item to choose, but you have to pick one thing to change.

3. Write down your list of goals, like I did because of Lou Holtz, then take the list and have it laminated in a wallet or pocket size. It costs fifty cents to do this at FedEx Kinko's. The most effective lists have your goals on them, the "no" list we talked about in Chapter 1, and a picture of something important to you on the other side, as a reminder of what's at stake. I have my family picture on mine.

4. Give a copy of that laminated list to somebody close to you—a spouse, a best friend—and ask them to help keep you on track toward your goals. You're going to feel more accountable for what you do when you know somebody will call you on your mistakes.

5. When you come up with your list of goals, e-mail it to me at goals@bryandodge.com. I read and answer every e-mail I get. Within forty-eight hours of reading this chapter, send me your no list and I will e-mail you a gift.

6. Review your list in the morning when you wake up and at night before you go to bed every day for the next twenty-one days. Just like sticking a picture of the skinny you on the refrigerator reminds you to stick to a diet, reviewing your lists keeps your goals fresh in your mind and reminds you of the successes you're seeing along the way.

Rule
7

Be a Leader

Everybody leads.

If you're a parent or some kind of manager at your business, you definitely know that's true. But don't think this chapter doesn't apply to you if you're not a manager or if you live by yourself and don't have any children.

When I give a talk at corporations about leadership, I start by asking those in the audience to raise their hands if they have people who report to them at work. Usually, about a tenth of the group raises their hands. After that, I ask if they actually talk to other living, breathing people. After a laugh, everybody raises a hand.

The truth is, if you're living in this world, you're responsible for being a leader for *somebody*. It could be somebody obvious like a child or a team of employees working for you. But you also provide leadership for your friends, your brother or sister, and for the people in your community. Even if it seems we're all self-sufficient people who are happy just to go home at night and hide away behind our fences and front doors, the world doesn't really work that way—even if it *seems* as if the Internet is trying to prevent us from ever having to talk to a person again, in person.

To live The Good Life, you have to be able to learn and grow with the help of the people around you, and you have to take responsibility for helping the people around you do the same. It isn't a deal you get to opt out of when it suits you.

I'm not going to downplay the gravity of that responsibility. It's probably the biggest one we all face from day to day. What could be more important than the relationships we have with the people who are closest to us? The skills it takes to be a leader aren't complicated or mysterious; they're rooted in common sense. They all start with what I call the Three Laws of Leadership.

I didn't invent these laws. They didn't come from some high-level symposium on leadership at an Ivy League business school. They come from years of experience interacting with people across the country who are hurting. Every single week, I stand in front of groups filled with people who are suffering because they've lost faith in the leadership of the companies at which they work. Or they've lost the ability to be leaders in their own lives—either in the office or at home. Or they just want to take their leadership skills to the next level.

Like an emergency room doctor who's seen too many motorcycle riders come in with serious injuries because they didn't wear a helmet, I've been in a lot of conference rooms at organizations where the leadership issues have done tremendous damage to both the people and the business.

But you can learn leadership. And if you've been a leader but lost your way, you can get it back.

The Three Laws of Leadership

If you walk down the personal development or business aisle at your local bookstore, you'll notice stacks and stacks of books that are devoted to the topic of leadership. In a way, that makes sense, because the subject is so important for both businesses and families.

But in an effort to help people, I believe many of the authors of those books have made the subject too complicated. By couching it in jargon and making it seem as if you need the equivalent of an MBA to understand it, they've almost removed it from the day-to-day life of the average person.

I believe that becoming an effective leader is a challenge, but it's one that anyone—*anyone*—can master. If you can understand and follow the Three Laws of Leadership I'm going to describe to you here, you can be an effective leader.

When You're Put in Charge, Take Charge

Sounds simple, right? But most people don't take the step that's most basic when it comes to leadership: accepting authority.

We've all seen managers who don't set the agenda in the office. And we've all seen parents who can't—or won't—control a misbehaving child. In both cases, the lack of leadership stems from the same cause, the unwillingness to accept authority.

For an ineffective manager in a business setting, that unwillingness is usually tied to two factors: an accountability aversion and a communication deficit. In simpler terms, some people in a leadership position don't want the responsibility that comes with it because they don't want to be blamed for a failure. Or, they've accepted the responsibility but can't—or won't—figure out a way to communicate the message to the rest of the team. If nobody can hear or understand you, you're not in charge.

So many parents have trouble being leaders at home because they are confused about what their relationship with their children should be. Should it be a loving, unconditional relationship? Of course. We all would do virtually anything to make sure our children were safe, and to ensure a great future for them. Would it be great to be buddies with your kids, and laugh and enjoy life together? Absolutely. My best days are spent out on the lake, waterskiing with my kids.

But being an effective leader at home means you're going to make decisions that the people you lead aren't always going to like. That's just as true in the living room as it is in the boardroom. And many, many parents of today grew up in ultra-strict households. They remember how much they disliked getting lectured and punished. They want their kids to like them—to the point where getting the kids to like them is more important than helping them develop into responsible adults.

Will you make mistakes? Of course. We all do. But the act of taking responsibility for your role as a leader is the most important thing you can do. It shows the people you're leading that you're invested in what happens. They can disagree with your methods, or your style of communication, but you will have made clear what your end goals are. That alone helps clarify any situation in a profound way.

It Never Gets Better than the Interview

It doesn't matter whether you're interviewing somebody for an entry-level sales job in your company or sitting nervously in a restaurant on a first date. The truth of both situations is that the person sitting across from you is trying hard to make a good impression. If you don't feel there's a good fit with that person right away, you need to go in a different direction.

You may be tempted to say to yourself, "I see so much potential in this person, and I can make him a fit for what I need." But the truth is, the person you see before you is the person you will have to deal with. If you determine that he or she is a good fit, either for the job or in your life, then start thinking ahead. But if that person is not what you're looking for, move on.

I'll never forget the last time I didn't listen to my own advice about it not getting better than the interview. I was looking for a new member for the team at my company, and "J. A." had everything I was looking for—a degree from a great college and some impressive work experience. He didn't have any background in the position I needed to fill, but I was sure he was a bright enough guy—and I was a good enough leader—to get him up to speed very quickly.

Before I brought him on board, I took him out to dinner with his wife, and my wife, Margaret. When we got home that night, I expected Margaret to tell me she thought he was great.

"I just don't feel right about him," she said.

My jaw just dropped. I sputtered that she didn't understand the business like I did, and that he was perfect for the job.

I don't have to tell you what happened next. I ignored Margaret's advice and hired Ted. Within a year, he cost me more money than I can even admit in this book. He almost cost me my company.

Learn two things from my mistake. First, realize that when you meet people who want a relationship with you—whether they're looking for a job, or a first date—they're showing you their best side. If something isn't clicking at that point, it's doubtful that it ever will.

Second, be willing to listen to other opinions. People who know you and understand you might see things that you don't, and can give you guidance. Letting your pride get in the way of that advice, or feeling like your success and power will override the truth is a dangerous mistake—and many, many leaders have learned this the expensive way, like I did.

If you do follow the advice here and pick the *person* before you pick the position, you'll have the chance to be rewarded in ways you didn't expect.

When I was coaching my youngest son's youth soccer team, a tiny kid came up to me before practice. He was only as tall as my waist, but about as wide as I was. He said that his friends on my team said that if any coach would let him play, it'd be me.

I asked him if he wanted to play soccer.

"Yes."

I asked him if he had ever played before.

"I was on a team, but the coach never played me. He said I wasn't fast enough, and I couldn't control the ball."

I don't know if you know anything about soccer, but those are pretty much the two most important skills to have. At that point, I decided that if I was going to put Joe on the team—and I believe that every kid should get a chance to be on a team—I wasn't going to do the same thing the other coaches did and make him sit all the time.

He was never going to be a scorer or a midfielder, but defense was a possibility because for kids that age, it was more about herding the kids with the ball in the right direction.

I asked Joe if he had ever herded cattle.

He was a super quiet kid, but he laughed.

"No."

"It's easy. You get on the left side of them and they go to the right. You get on the right side of them and they go to the left. But if you get too close, you'll spook them. It's all about distance and angle."

Joe didn't have very much speed, but he got the concept of herding right away. He was great at not letting the faster players suck him in close and then pivot around them. He was, literally, an expert at getting in the way.

The next practice, nobody could get by Joe. He either herded the player with the ball toward the middle, where he had help from other defenders, or he herded them out of bounds.

When it came time for the first game, the kids voted on who would be captain. It was Joe. Joe's parents were in the stands, and they had tears in their eyes when they heard the chants from the sidelines, "Nobody gets by Mo Joe."

Joe had finally found a place where he could be himself, and people believed in him. He was in a position where he could use what he could do, not get criticized for what he *couldn't* do.

That game, Joe was matched up with the other team's quickest player. He did his thing and shut that player down for the entire sixty minutes. Joe came to the sidelines when the final whistle blew and he was just ecstatic. I've never seen a kid happier, and I couldn't have been happier for him.

When Joe came to the team, we had been looking for what every other soccer team is looking for—fast kids who could handle the ball. I'm glad we could see past that obvious need and get to what Joe needed, because we both wound up winning.

As a leader—in your office, with your friends, or in your family—your responsibility is to put people where they can succeed, not in the most convenient slot. Then, you need to get out of the way and let them.

If You Can't Change the People, Change the People

Admit it. A person's name just popped into your head. It's the person at your office who just refuses to be a productive part of the team, no matter how much coaching or encouragement you give. Or the person who's been a part of your life for years but has a long track record of betraying your trust or letting you down.

If you've reached the point where you just can't get to someone, you have to do what's best for everybody and make a change. That's a relatively straightforward thing to do in work life. Sometimes, it's just not a good match between a person and a job, or a person and the rest of the people on the team. Most of the time, *everybody* feels better once a change is made—even the person who is losing his or her job. The key thing to understand is that if you *don't* make a change, the people around you see that you aren't willing to do anything to solve a problem, and you lose your ability to lead. You've lost the trust of the people you're leading, and they'll only follow to the extent that they're required to, not because they want to.

What happens when it's a family member who won't change? That's obviously a more sensitive, exceptionally painful situation. You can go out and find another job. You can't just go out and replace your children or your parents. Once you've accepted that there is a problem in the relationship and communicated to everyone in the family about it, you need to have a group meeting—with everyone—to address it. If the person is willing to change, you have to give him or her your unqualified support. And if the person wants to change but can't, you need to provide access to the necessary professional help.

If the person refuses to change, then you have to make a decision as a family. You can either live with it, or you need to let the person go. That could mean a divorce, or placing a child in a different live-away environment, or in the case of a sibling or older parent, deciding that you won't be a part of his or her life anymore.

Is that harsh? Yes and no. Yes, because you don't want to have to break those bonds. But as a parent and a leader, your job is to protect *all* the people in the family. And you can't—as much as you love an individual in the family—let one person jeopardize the health and security of the rest of the family. It's heartbreaking, but true.

How to Become a Better Leader

Leadership is helping people learn the lessons they need to learn, even if they aren't always comfortable ones. Anybody can hand out the bonus checks or announce that the family is taking a vacation. Leadership is about giving people compassion, consistency, and, most important, belief.

If you're looking to become a better leader in any part of your life, I don't think anything I've said so far has been a surprise. What makes great leaders great is that they use consistent, commonsense approaches even under the most stressful conditions.

The next question, though, is the obvious one—and the one I get from a lot of people who have just heard me speak at a corporate leadership day. If you've recognized that you want to be a better leader and you're inspired to change, *how* do you do it? How do you develop the skills you need?

First, ask yourself why you've decided to build your leadership skills. What was the wake-up call? I've found that the people who have the most success growing into better leaders are the ones who are inspired by a particular event—a crisis at work, or reaching the end of their rope with a child or a spouse.

If you're deciding to develop your leadership skills because of an article you read in the newspaper, or because it sounds like something interesting to do, you're going to struggle. Because until you've reached the point where you can say to yourself, "I've had enough, and I have to change," it's going to be very easy to drift away from the work that this process requires.

Next, ask yourself how your closest friend would describe the way you are *today*. He may have known you for twenty-five years and think you're a great person overall, but he may also have an opinion about the person you've been for the last twelve months. Would your closest friend think you were a person of integrity, or would he think you've been slipping lately?

Why is this important? Because before you can be an effective leader—in small situations or big ones—you need to know who you are and where you stand *today*. If you're in a position where you're trying to please too many people—and we've all been there—you get into what I call a gray zone. In all the compromises you make for other people, you start to lose who you really are—and the people around you don't recognize you anymore.

The first step is to use the perspective of somebody who has known you for a long time to get back to the baseline of who you really are. Start with integrity from that point, and you're on the way to taking ownership of leadership in your life. Integrity is like the rebar in concrete. Without the rebar, the concrete falls apart when it gets put under stress.

"Ownership of leadership" is kind of a mouthful, but I really believe it's the single skill we each need to master to make our lives—and our community—great. It's that important. If you don't have ownership of the leadership in your life, you can't have it for anybody else. Not for your children, your spouse, or your friends; and not for the people who work for you or with you.

The following are six concrete ways you can get started owning leadership in your own life—today.

Keep Your Promises

It sounds simple, but in practice, it will change how you live your life. If you hold yourself to all your promises, you'll stop promising so much. Once you stop promising so much, you remove the stress that comes from disappointing people when you don't deliver. This isn't some kind of free pass to stop making promises altogether; the important people in your life are going to need assurances from time to time. I'm talking about using words when you should be using actions. Don't promise to be at your son's game and then miss it because of work. Say you'll be there, and then show up.

I was coaching my soccer team, and one of my players—his nickname was "Big Foot"—was having a fantastic game. He scored a goal, but instead of celebrating with his teammates, he looked over at the parking lot. I figured out that his dad must have promised him that he was going to be at the game.

After we had won—thanks to Big Foot's goals—and were filing off the field, a car pulled into the lot. It was Big Foot's dad. He came over to me and apologized for missing the game, saying he got tied up at work.

"Don't tell me," I said. "Tell him."

"It's okay. He'll understand," the dad said.

No, he won't.

All a child knows is that you didn't do what you said you were going to do. If you tell your son you won't be able to make the game, he'll understand that. But breaking your promise is something else entirely.

Stop Blaming

One of my closest friends, the author David Cottrell, told me something about blame that I never forgot. Blame is looking backward. Responsibility is looking to the future. I remember watching a movie in which a young boy and girl were crossing the desert with a native guide. They got halfway across, and one boy sat down in the sand and stared at the tracks they had left behind them. The guide came over and said, "Unless that is your future, I wouldn't spend too much time focusing on it." Choose to focus on the things you can control going forward—and not the unfortunate things that happened in the past.

Focus on the things you can control and you'll stay in control. If you focus on the things you can't, you'll pull yourself out of control. It's your choice.

Change the Way You Walk

Believe it or not, your mood and attitude respond to the way you carry yourself. If you slump your shoulders and walk tentatively, your emotions conform to that negative frame. Pull your shoulders back and lean slightly forward when you walk. Concentrate on having good posture for the next two days—even if it sounds corny—and I'll bet you the price of this book that you'll feel more positive and energized.

Share Your Mistakes

We have this tremendously misguided idea about "strength" in leadership—that a leader never shows weakness. I believe in strong leadership, but I don't believe that people should pretend they don't make mistakes. That's just as true for a department manager as it is for a parent. If you show the people around you that their mistakes—the honest kind, not the sloppy kind—are going to be severely punished while yours are going to be ignored, you'll lose their respect and trust. Besides, the most productive discoveries and breakthroughs in the world didn't pop into existence perfect and fully formed. A lot of sweat, scrap paper, do-overs, and busted deadlines went into every single one.

I like to say mistakes are the great fertilizer in your life. They can help you—and the people around you—grow if you share them and use them to find The Good Life.

Embrace the Role Model Job

Sometimes, you're a role model whether you like it or not—when it comes to your children, for example. They'll learn more from what they see you do than from what you say. But most people don't realize that they're just as much of a role model in the rest of life—for other family members, friends, and coworkers—even if the relationship isn't as well-defined as the parent-child one is. If you live your life with openness, integrity, and a positive attitude, a number of things will result. Obviously, you're going to feel better about yourself and have more confidence. That's Personal Development 101. But there's a more subtle force at play, too. If you embrace the responsibility of being a role model, your relationships with family members and coworkers will change for the better. If you're straightforward and open, the people in your life will give you the benefit of the doubt when you make mistakes. They'll treat you with the respect you've shown them as a role model.

Find Your True Talent

This piece of advice is important no matter where you sit on the leadership spectrum, but it's particularly important if you're managing a business or a home. It's very difficult to be great at something that isn't your true talent or calling. Sure, there are professional athletes blessed with fantastic skills who can succeed even if they don't have a burning love for their sport. But for the rest of us, that's a tall order. If you can find your true talent—and I'll give you more information about how to do that in the next section—you accomplish two things. First, it makes it easier for you to commit the time and energy it takes to do a job well. Second, it lessens the tendency to envy others for what they have. If you aren't satisfied or well-matched to what you're doing, you're naturally going to look at—and resent—what other people have or do.

The more comfortable you are with yourself, the more willing you're going to be to let others be who they are. Great managers—at home and at work—understand what they excel at and take on that task, and they delegate the things others can do better. At my house, it certainly works that way. My wife is a teacher, so when it comes time to help with homework, who do you think gets the call? It isn't me. On the other hand, I enjoy being outside a lot more than Margaret does, so when it's time to show the kids how to ride a horse or build a barn or how to water-ski, that's my area of expertise. Does that mean Margaret isn't involved in those things, or that I'm not involved in helping with homework? Of course not. We each play a part—sharing responsibility—but whoever is better at a particular task takes the lead.

I once interviewed a very sharp woman for a position at my company, and I asked her why she wanted the position. She paused for a second, and it looked like she was trying to come up with a politically correct answer. Finally, she simply said, "I don't know."

She had a terrific résumé, and the answer surprised me, so I followed up. "Okay, if you could pick whatever you wanted to be in life, and the moment you picked it, you'd be the best at it, what would you choose to be?"

"A missionary," she answered.

One of my friends in Dallas recruits missionaries for work in Africa, and I gave her his number. She met with him, and she's been doing that work for twelve years now.

She found her true calling. My job wasn't to try to *get* something from her, for my company. It was to *give* something to her, to help her find her true place.

Do You Know Who You Are?

When I'm giving a presentation, I often wrap it up with a simple question. I ask the audience, "Do you know who you are?"

The response is interesting. Some people laugh. They think it's a silly question, and for them, maybe it is. Maybe they're very self-confident and know exactly what they want out of life and how they fit in. They're also pretty rare.

For most people, the question "Do you know who you are?" is a simple one, but also troubling. Many people are on a particular path in their profession or in their family life, and they *hope*—rather than are *convinced*—that it's the right one.

Maybe you feel that your job is just that—a job, something you're required to go to every day to pay the bills. Maybe you feel that your family life isn't what you want it to be, because you're at a loss about how to fix some of the problems you face. Those issues are difficult to face when you're not sure where your starting point is.

Football is a great analogy for what I'm talking about here. If you were starting a team from scratch, you could map out all the different positions on the field, and you could make plans to fill those positions with different kinds of players. Running backs would be quick and elusive. Quarterbacks would be great decision-makers with strong arms. Linemen would be big and strong, with good footwork.

But when it comes to filling the positions in your life, the benchmarks aren't so straightforward. For many people, it's not so obvious if they're a running back, a quarterback, or a lineman. And if you're cast in the wrong role, two things happen, and both of them are bad. One, you don't perform as well as somebody who is right for the role, and two, you're unhappy because you're miscast.

You've got to do a lot of soul-searching about who you are and what you want to be, and there's no simple, magic-bullet answer. But there *is* a way to get some guidance and to find the right place to start.

You've probably taken a personality test like the Myers-Briggs at one time or another. The results may have been interesting or entertaining, but they probably didn't tell you much that you didn't already know.

I've done a lot of work with Ken Channell, who came up with a different kind of test, called Talent DNA, which I think is one of the best ways to identify the important traits that make you who you are. More important, I believe it helps you focus on the things in your life—and in your job—that satisfy you and contribute to your happiness.

The sixty multiple-choice questions on the quick online test provide insight into the talents and interests that really inspire you—and provide a guide to finding situations that fit those talents and interests. The test breaks down your personality into three categories—how you think about things, how you feel about them, and how you act on them—and provides examples and professional scenarios that would be both positive and negative for you. I've included a copy of my test results here, so you can see what I mean.

●●● The Talent DNA Assessment Results for Bryan Dodge

OVERVIEW				
Assessment	Red	Yellow	Blue	Green
Drive	8	3	3	6
kNowledge	4	8	5	3
Advantage	8	6	6	0
Talent DNA Totals	20	17	14	9

DRIVE			
Red	Yellow	Blue	Green
8	3	3	6

Feeling: You come with your own unique wiring that is basically your survival instincts. It is why you do the things you do. When you are highly stressed or threatened, you act from this emotional part of your Talent DNA. This person has these feelings at the Drive level:

Red 8

- Bryan, you have a need to win.
- No matter how much you have achieved and how old you are, you feel that you should have achieved more by now.
- You are competitive and you naturally take charge of any situation you encounter.
- You are in a hurry to get where you are going.
- Bryan, you are money motivated and you measure your success by how much you make and have.
- You have a survival instinct to protect yourself.
- You have a need to feel like you are getting something done.
- When you have a hammer, everything is a nail and just needs to be hit harder.

- Often, you are confident you can knock your way out of whatever trouble you get into by just doing the next thing.

Green 6

- Bryan, you have a need to analyze your situation based on the past.
- Since you need consistency, predictability, and stability, you do not like change.
- You have a need to avoid making the same mistake twice.
- You also have a need to put everything in a box and to have control over what happens to you.
- You believe that everyone makes mistakes, but Bryan, if you make the same mistake twice, it is not a good day.
- You analyze every new situation to determine what about it is similar to a situation in the past when you made a mistake.
- You need to avoid rushing because your experience tells you that when you rush you make mistakes and that is not good.

KNOWLDEGE			
Red	**Yellow**	**Blue**	**Green**
4	8	5	3

Thinking: By the time you are five or six years old, you have developed a second level of your Talent DNA based on the input you have received from your parents or the people you were with in those early years. This is what you think you "OUGHT TO DO." How you prefer to communicate and how you learn. This person has these thoughts at the kNowledge level:

Yellow 8

- Bryan, you think you should be involved.
- If someone needs your help, there is almost nothing you will not do in response to that request.

- You will climb walls and leap over buildings if you think the team needs your help.
- You work best with management that is flexible and has broad goals. Bryan, you thrive on being part of the team.
- You have confidence in consensus.
- You place a high value on the right to participate and to be involved.
- You do not respond well to rigid bureaucratic leadership.
- Bryan, you learn best by watching someone complete the project before you start.
- You respond best to democratic leadership that bases decisions on the consensus of the team.

Blue 5

- Bryan, you think you should have input.
- You like to be asked, "What do you think about this?"
- You can detect listener insincerity when you are telling someone your ideas.
- You like to play intellectual pitch. You throw out an idea and learn as much from the response as from the original idea.
- Bryan, other people often mistake that you are saying this is what we are going to do . . . and not what if we did this.
- You think you should have the freedom to manage yourself.
- Bryan, you are directed by ideas and inspiration.
- You flourish under indirect management where your ideas are sought after.
- You have a tendency to follow your own thoughts about things.
- You are always asking why and what if.
- Your goal is to think of a better way to do things or a way to improve a situation.
- You thrive on asking questions and see that as a right and not a privilege.

- Since you place a high value on ideas, you think you should have as many as possible.
- You do not respond well to being told what to do since that limits your possibilities.

ADVANTAGE			
Red	**Yellow**	**Blue**	**Green**
8	6	6	0

Performing: Around age fourteen you have developed a Talent DNA that gives you an Advantage. It is this level that you enjoy being in. When you are performing using your Advantage, you are functioning at your best. This will always give you an advantage if you can spend 75 percent of your day using this part of your Talent DNA. This person has these talents and strengths at the Advantage level:

Red 8

- Bryan, you can ignore everything around you when you see an opportunity to win and get results.
- You enjoy being direct and can offend people with less Red without being aware of it, since directness comes naturally to you.
- You enjoy getting things done. You are energized by checking things off your list.
- Bryan, you have a talent to focus all of your energy on what you are doing and you are good at doing a single project at a time.
- You prefer to lead by example; you say just do something.
- Your ability to be direct can come across as abrasive and dictatorial. Because you are focused, you can appear to act impulsively.
- Your comfort with doing the next thing accounts for you coming across as demanding.
- You have an urgency about what you do.

Yellow 6

- Bryan, you enjoy working with and relating to people.
- You are comfortable organizing and coordinating with people.
- You have a talent for relating to other people and look for the things you have in common in order to build relationships.
- You are comfortable engaging each individual and building consensus among the members of a team.
- You look for opportunities to help other people since you are most comfortable when you are involved with others.
- Because of your ability to identify with others, Bryan, you are good in communication-oriented roles.
- You ask yourself, how can I persuade all these people to work together?
- You enjoy being flexible and you are good at adapting to the opinions and thoughts of others.
- You can usually find some common ground with almost everyone you meet.
- Teamwork comes naturally to you, Bryan.
- Since your focus is on receiving recognition from the team, Bryan, you know that you must be a team player and get others on the team.
- You look for the strengths of others and find ways to incorporate their strengths to benefit the team.

Blue 6

- Bryan, you enjoy solving problems since that gives you the opportunity to use your skills at asking why and what-if.
- You have a talent to evaluate alternative solutions to a problem.
- You prefer to consider alternative ways of doing things.
- You enjoy the challenge of using your mind to find a better way to accomplish something.

- You tend to focus on innovation and should avoid being put in the role of maintaining the innovation or solution.
- You are creative in your approach to everything.
- Your management style tends to be indirect since you are usually thinking about an idea or a solution rather than what others are doing.
- Bryan, you are usually planning and coming up with alternatives rather than focusing on what is going on at the moment.
- You enjoy counseling others since it gives you an opportunity to solve a problem.
- In the process of thinking about how to solve a problem, you can develop solutions that will not work.
- This does not frustrate you since it was just another possibility, but Bryan, it can frustrate others who are looking to you to solve their problem.

When I completed my questionnaire, I was blown away by two things. First, I was impressed with how accurately it pegged the subtleties of my personality—how, for example, I like to win but also have a desire for consistency and predictability. Second, it told me that the way I think about things is opposite of the way I *feel* about them. In other words, the way I consciously process concrete information—looking for a structured way to solve a problem—is different from my visceral emotional reaction to things, my wanting to have control over a situation.

The results went a long way toward helping me tailor my professional life around the things I do well and enjoy—like interacting with people—and eliminate or outsource the parts I didn't enjoy, like the business development and management end.

I'm a big believer in the Talent DNA program, and I recommend it at the end of all my presentations. For more information on it and a free preview of how it works, you can go to my website, Bryan Dodge.com, and click on the link at the top right of the page.

The Qualities of a Great Leader

A few years ago, I was asked to play in a charity golf tournament to benefit cancer research. Now, I'm not the greatest golfer. As a matter of fact, whenever I'm invited to play, I make a point to tell my hosts that they haven't made a bag big enough to carry all the balls I'm going to need for eighteen holes. But I enjoy it, and I enjoy spending time outside and meeting new people.

At this tournament, I was paired with a guy who is extremely successful. He's probably the wealthiest person I've ever met.

He also had the biggest temper. For six holes, he threw one big, extended tantrum—either about his shot, or about the pace of play, or about anything else that came into his field of vision.

There comes a time when you have to take the lead and try to make a positive change in someone else's life, so I got up my courage and called the man aside.

"Would you mind if I give you a piece of advice?" I asked him.

He bored a hole straight through me with his eyes.

"I don't take advice from too many people, but you've helped me in my business and with my family," he said.

I took that as a yes.

"You're not good enough to get that mad," I said, laughing a little to show I wasn't trying to be mean. "If you're going to suck at golf, at least have a good time."

He gave me a startled look, as if that had never occurred to him before.

"The scorecard has a small box for your score, because there's no room to put an excuse in there," I said. "It doesn't say I made an eight, but it was raining. It just says eight. Which means you suck."

Leaders understand that very powerful principle better than anybody else. They live with a very small box for the score. There's no room in it to make excuses. Either you succeeded or you didn't, and it's up to you to understand what went right or wrong and learn from it for the next time.

And, ironically, the less room you give yourself for making excuses, the *more* room the people around you will give you when you make a mistake. Because they know you're harder on yourself than they could ever be.

At the risk of sounding like one of those cheesy motivational posters you see on the wall of the empty cubicle down the hall, I want to tell you about the qualities I believe make a good leader. And I think they're anything but cheesy. They're critical characteristics that most of the great leaders I've been around have shared.

1. Potential. Everyone starts out as an awkward beginner. It's where you go from there that tells of your leadership potential. Leaders push themselves to get better, even when it's easier to quit.

2. Dedication. I'd love to put a giant headline on the cover of this book that says you can become a wonderful parent, friend, and employee in thirty minutes, just by reading this book, but it wouldn't be true. There are no shortcuts. You have to be willing to pay the price to get to where you want to go, and dedication is the measure of the cost.

3. Preparation. Most of us aren't good enough to get away with haphazard preparation for our work life or home life. I know I'm not. Make a commitment to stop winging it and your job will go back to working for you, instead of the other way around.

4. Courage. Courage is the one thing most negative people try to take from you in life—because it's easier for them to live with themselves if they don't see you succeeding. That's why you're more likely to see people trying to tear down a successful person rather than kick somebody who's already down. The bright side? If somebody is trying to take your courage to stand up for what you believe, it means you're in a good place.

5. Concentration. Focus is everything. It's the measure of where you're dedicating your effort and attention. You're never going to be as effective when you split your attention. That's why I'm such a big believer in work-home balance—which we're going to talk about in the next chapter. When you're at work, be at work. When you're home, be at home.

Nobody knows more than I do how difficult staying focused can be sometimes. One of the biggest challenges in my life has been staying focused enough to see a task through to the end. My parents tried to help me with ADHD medication, but this was back in the 1970s, when we didn't know as much about the disorder as we do now.

What really helped was my parents teaching me to become "addicted" to finishing what I started. The rule was that I couldn't start something if I wasn't going to finish it. If my job was to go out and build a fence, I had to stick with the job until it was done. The need to follow through became almost a compulsion for me, and it drives me to this day.

They say the apple doesn't fall far from the tree, and my three children all have the same challenge when it comes to paying attention. We sat down with them and told them about drugs like Adderall, which help with concentration, and they tried them to see what it felt like. But my point to them has always been that society pays for results, and if you can get those without relying on a pill, you're better off—a pill is never a replacement for a skill. I'm proud to say that with hard work, they've all been successful without the medication.

6. Perspective. You can excel in all these categories and still fall short as a leader if you don't have perspective. It's the most important thing of all, because it's what connects you to other people. Perspective is understanding your relationship to the people around you and to the world, and having a sense for the relative importance of things. You can be the most exacting boss or parent in the world, but the people you lead will respect you only if they understand that you have their world in perspective—that you know that making a small mistake isn't the same thing as pitching the company into bankruptcy.

It doesn't matter if you're a college football coach, the CEO of a business, or a parent with two kids at home. If you can master these skills, you're going to be successful.

Forty-Eight-Hour Action Plan

1. Write down two things you haven't taken charge of in your life and commit to acting on them. It could be transferring the balance on a high-interest credit card, or having a conversation with your child about homework skills. Whatever the things you choose, commit to taking action within two days.

2. Choose to look both ways. When you're presented with a leadership challenge at work or at home, commit to carefully examining the issue from both sides. Even if you don't end up agreeing with the other person's position, you'll gain perspective about how they think, and show them that you're listening.

3. Write down your "wake-up call"—the single thing that makes you want to change and take ownership of leadership—and put it in a place where you can see it. My wake-up call was realizing that it wasn't somebody else's job to take care of my family's needs. It was mine. I laminated a piece of paper with "Delegate the things that aren't important!" on it and taped it to the dash of my truck. I see it every time I head for the office or the airport.

4. Do not commit to a relationship personally or professionally until you have defined the talents and qualities of the other person. In other words, know what you're getting into. As I've said in other chapters, it's okay to say no.

Rule
8

Find the Balance Between Work and Home

There's no such thing as work-home balance.

That might be a strange way to start a chapter called "Find the Balance Between Work and Home," but there really is no such thing.

I meet with corporate leaders every week, and I'm asked many of the same questions again and again. The CEOs want to know how to help their employees have more "work-home balance" because they think it's a magic formula for increased productivity.

If you're happy, are you going to be a better employee? Absolutely. Are you going to be better at being a dad or a mom or a friend? Of course. Does it have anything to do with punching a time clock, or the number of hours you work in a week? No way.

There's no such thing as an artificially created "balance." There isn't some formula you can plug in that says you need to be at work for eight hours, then at home for ten before you can work another eight hours. It'd be nice if the real world was orderly that way, but we all know it isn't.

In real life, you're always either heading for a crisis or coming out of one. That's just as true for a Fortune 500 company as it is for a family. My own family had to deal with health crises that included two blown-out knees and a broken back in a thirty-six-month period.

The balance that comes in The Good Life is more like the kind you use to ride a bike. You're always pedaling, and if you start to tip a little bit to the left, you lean right to restore your equilibrium. If you overcorrect, then you need to lean a little more to the left to get back in balance.

In this chapter, I'm going to show you how to become more sensitive to where you sit in relation to a balanced life, and more confident about your ability to change where you sit.

The Fallacy of Scheduling

At this point, you might be saying to yourself, "You don't know my business, Bryan. It seems like my work responsibilities never end." You feel like you'll never have a big enough shovel for the hole you have to dig.

I do know how a person can feel that way. I felt overwhelmed in my own life for a long time. I even used to have to take my kids to my office on weekends so I could do some work, while they wandered up and down the halls. There just didn't seem to be enough hours in the day.

And as for modern technology, cell phones, Blackberries, wireless Internet, and e-mail have just made the problem worse. The whole idea behind those machines is that they're supposed to save us time, but for most people they don't. Instead, they become a kind of high-tech anchor, demanding more and more time. Twenty years ago, you couldn't exchange e-mails with a client across the country—or across the world—at 8 P.M. on a Tuesday. You had to wait until you could get to the office and send a fax or, God forbid, a letter.

I'm not against technology. I've got all those gadgets I just mentioned, and two of some of them. And there's no doubt that they can make you productive if—and it's a big if—they're used properly. What do I mean by that?

It's simple. You have to take responsibility for your time. You have to use those technological tools to actually make you more efficient, not keep you chained to your work twenty-four hours a day. There's nothing worse than playing golf with a guy who's holding a cell phone to his ear while he's putting.

If you let technology—and the misguided drive for "productivity"—control you instead, you're falling for what I call the Fallacy of Scheduling.

If you let your work control you in that way, and if you keep saying to yourself, "I'm going to make just one more call, even though I said I'd be home before seven," you're losing sight of what The Good Life is. If you committed to a big organizational meeting with your team at work, and you decide to play hooky so you can hang out with your son, you've also lost sight of what The Good Life is. Your job is not to work more hours nor is it to break your promises to the people in your professional life so that you can spend every moment at home. Your job is to get done what needs to be done—both at work and at home—with the time you have. It's not a matter of finding more space on the schedule. It's a matter of picking the right things to be on the schedule and having them on there at the right times.

Let me say that again in a different way, because it's probably something you haven't heard before: The truth about life is that you're going to miss some soccer games every once in awhile. You're going to have to take rain checks on dinners with your wife or beers with your buddies. You're going to pass on sales trips because you committed to taking the kids to Disneyland. And you're going to leave work an hour early to see the first-round play-off soccer game.

To live The Good Life, you need to have a balance between work and home. One doesn't come at the expense of the other. If you're not happy at work, the people you live with are going to pay for that. If you're not happy at home, you're not going to be very productive at work.

Being home with my family is a big priority in my life. I spend less than forty nights away from home per year, even though I give more than three hundred talks across North America. I make it my priority to do my work and get home as soon as I can. But when I'm on the road, talking to a group of three hundred realtors in Cleveland, I'm fully committed to giving them everything I have. And when I rush back to the airport so I can catch the 5:40 flight to Dallas, I'm getting home so I can fully commit that time to my wife and kids.

Don't fall for the Fallacy of Scheduling. Commit to being where you are when you're there, and using all the tools at your disposal to make the most efficient use of your time.

You should always be striving to know where you fall on the work-home balance meter, and have a sense of what you need to do to get the meter moving back toward the middle.

Four Simple Steps to Finding Your Balance

Sounds great, right? But how do you find the balance I'm talking about? You find it by doing more things on purpose instead of letting them happen to you—and taking a more active, vocal role in the things in your life that affect you.

Remember the no list we talked about in Chapter 1—the one where you decided what things you just weren't going to subject yourself to anymore? Here's where a new kind of no list is really going to get a workout. I decided I wasn't going to cut my own grass anymore, because I preferred to have the three hours it took me to do it to spend with my kids, on the lake. At work, I decided that when a company booked me for a day, I wasn't going to make any schedule changes if a larger booking came looking for the same date later. Why? First of all, it isn't right to do that to the smaller booking. Second, it would mean juggling dates and disrupting time with my family.

Those are pretty specific examples, but the skills you're going to need to find your own balance are very straightforward. I know you have them. You just have to find them. Here are the four steps to doing just that:

Make Your List

Unfortunately, most people live life in a reactive mode. Things happen, and they do their best to respond. Sometimes that's "enough" to get by, but a lot of times it isn't. Is it any wonder, then, that so many people are so stressed out? Living your life like a constant fire drill isn't healthy, and it certainly isn't productive.

You have to start designing your life. That means, when you get to the end of a workday, you make a list of the things you want to accomplish the next day, while you have your current day fresh in your mind. Then, when you come in, you've got a plan.

The same holds true for your home life. When you get ready to go to bed, make another list of the things you want to accomplish at home the next day. Make sure the two lists—work and home—mesh in terms of the time commitment.

Does that mean everything is always going to go according to plan? Heck no. But you're going to be able to respond to challenges and surprises so much more easily if you have a plan and can see where your time and resources are committed.

One of the lessons in life I've learned the hard way is that if you *don't* make a list of what you want to happen tomorrow—whether it's on a legal pad next to your bed or in your head—you're almost guaranteed to be diverted into working off of somebody else's list. That's not always awful—when the person has your best interests in mind—but I don't think it's something you'd want to live with full time.

One of the most consistent comments I get from groups I speak to about making this list is that the act of doing it is in itself liberating. It makes people feel that they now have permission to say no to things that don't fit their goals or priorities. When you free yourself that way, you're in a position to perform so much better—at work and at home—and you leave yourself time to actually enjoy the surprises life throws at you. Some people I see are going such great guns to try to catch up and be "productive" that they miss the great things life has to offer, like taking the scenic route home or surprising their kid by coming home early and playing catch in the yard.

We talked in Rule Four about the idea of confronting issues on their time—meaning you need to make a step to resolve something that comes into your head within forty-eight hours, or you'll lose that push to ever get it done. As you're making your daily list of things you want to accomplish, the same principle of "on its time" applies. The people I know who have achieved great balance between work and home accomplish this because, at both places, they handle each list item and challenge on its time. They don't push a conversation with a client off to the next day when they can do it this morning. Why? Because they don't know what surprises could turn up tomorrow, and adding things that could be finished today to the queue for tomorrow just compounds the risk of getting overwhelmed down the road.

Are you going to be able to check everything off the list, every single day? No way. Sometimes, you can't avoid having to push something from today to the next day, and that's okay. But the list becomes like a batting average for a major league baseball player. Some days, you might strike out three times and go 0-for-5, but that doesn't change the goal of hitting .300 for the season.

Establish Your Priorities

Every time I speak to a group, I ask a few people to share their priorities and they almost always give the same answers: make more money, lose weight, or get a promotion at work. I think it's great that these folks have something in mind that they'd like to work on. But those things they're mentioning aren't *priorities*, they're goals—and there's a big difference.

Priorities are the foundation you build you goals on. They hold the goals together. A goal is a task or an achievement you want to accomplish—like losing twenty pounds, or earning $10,000 more this year. A priority is the big-picture motivation *behind* the goal. Priorities are the inspiration.

Before I can ask you what your goals are, I have to ask you about your priorities, because your priorities are going to drive your goals. Let me give you an example.

I told you before about the list of laminated goals I always keep in my wallet. Here are the first three things on that goal list right now:

1. Pay off my daughter's wedding before the wedding.
2. Get to 165 pounds.
3. Finish this book.

But when it comes to my priorities, that's a different kind of list. My top three priorities:

1. Spiritual
2. Family
3. Health

I always ask the people attending one of my seminars to send me their goal lists. I read every one, and it's amazing how often you see a money goal at the top. But if you asked the same person to come up with a priority list, money wouldn't be anywhere near the top.

To live The Good Life, your goal list and priority list have to relate to each other. They don't have to exactly match—because your short-term goals are going to change depending on your situation—but they have to work together. If there's a disconnect between them, you're going to struggle. And in the end, you won't succeed at either of them.

When I make my day-to-day list of things I want to accomplish, I'm using both of my lists to give weight to my schedule. If I know I have two big meetings tomorrow about a new radio contract and the launch of my website, that means 60 percent of my day is already spoken for. And since spending time with my family is always a top priority, I know that I'm not going to be able to commit to much more on the business side besides those two meetings. If my business partner wants to have a planning meeting, I know it needs to be a twenty-minute meeting, not a two-hour meeting. And if a friend calls me up and asks to have lunch, I'm going to have to say next week would be a better time.

If you develop a sense of what your goals and priorities are, you have a great tool to make decisions about how you spend your time, both day-to-day and in the big picture.

Dial In Your Focus

A few weeks ago, a man came up to me after one of my talks and told me he'd seen me speak eleven times. That just blew me away—and it made me a little worried that maybe he wasn't getting my message. But the more I talked to him, the more what he said made perfect sense. He told me that my jokes had gotten better over the years (which I appreciated), but more important, that every time he came and saw me, he came away from the day with more focus on the important things in life.

What does that mean? That we're always going to have to work at being committed and staying focused on what's important. It's not a trick you learn once and then just click it on autopilot. There are always things that are pulling at you in life and challenging you. Sometimes, you're going to lose focus—either intentionally or unintentionally—but you need to know how to get it back when you do.

I've been to dozens of time management seminars, and every time a speaker in one of them talks about how it's possible to achieve perfect balance, I have to laugh. It's impossible. You're always going to be pulled in one direction or another—work or home. The key is to dial in that focus and understand your priorities so you know where you fall on the scale at all times. That was a hard thing for me to do for a long time. I'd obsess over some problem at the office, then wrestle with it in my head all the way home and on into my time with my family. I knew that was something I was going to have to change if I wanted to be happy.

When you're going hard for work, be there 100 percent, but know that you need to go hard at home when you're done, to push the bar back to equal—at least temporarily. It's no different than going on a two-week vacation and leaving the Blackberry home. When you come back, you're going to have to spend extra time at the office returning e-mails and catching up on what you missed.

I've seen too many people get to that beach and spend the entire time obsessing about work. Then, when they get back to work, they daydream about what it's going to be like to take the next vacation at the beach. They were in the wrong place both times.

Is there a magic bullet to turning that focus back on again, either at work or home? No. It comes down to knowing why it's so important that you do. The consequences are more than you want to live with. It's a fear factor. If I don't choose to focus on my relationship with my wife, or with my kids, I'll lose those relationships. I could still have all the mechanical management responsibilities, like paying the bills and providing the roof over everybody's head, but I wouldn't be a dad, a person who is a real part of a relationship.

Check Off Your Wins

Once you've made your list and established your priorities, you've got to commit to "small wins" by checking those things off day by day. How many times have you made a mental note of the things you have to do each day, only to get sidetracked by some distraction that turned out not to be that important? Then, it's the end of the day and you feel like you're behind. What happens next? It's the family killer. You add more on to your list, and you take it home with you—either literally, by sitting at the kitchen table doing some report instead of hanging out with your kids, or figuratively, by coming home so worried about what you have to do tomorrow that you can't relax.

The answer isn't asking for less responsibility or less to do. Do you want to accomplish less, earn less, or have less? Asking for less hassle isn't going to work, either, unless you never want to be a friend, fall in love, or have a family.

The answer is to take the reins of your life day to day. Focus and knock those things off your list, one by one. It's an old joke, but it's true. How do you eat an elephant? One bite at a time. If you work on yourself and make these commitments, you can get back to having your job work for you—by giving you something stimulating and rewarding to experience every day, and a paycheck for your family—instead of you having to work for your job.

Protect Your "Balance Place"

In all the chapters in this book, I hope I've been able to show you the real differences between a short-term, Band-Aid fix and changing your life for good. Because the nature of Band-Aids is that they're only good for a short time—like a crash diet where the only thing you can eat is asparagus.

If you're going to make a lifetime commitment to understanding the balance between work and home and making it work for you, you have to make a plan that's going to give you the highest return on your energy. Because if you're fighting the plan every hour of every day and feel like you're just beaten up and drained, you're not going to be able to do it long term. That's just reality.

To get the highest return on your energy, you need to stop putting it places where it's drained but not replenished. The biggest drain is spending time with people who do nothing but take. At home, the code name we use for people who just take and don't give is "bad seed." You know one. It's a person who believes life owes him or her. If you're having a tough day, the bad seed is a person who gets perverse enjoyment out of that. It's a person who never owns up to mistakes. When things go wrong, it's always somebody else's fault. It goes without saying that if you have the option of staying away from people like that, you should.

Coworkers can be energy robbers. Maybe you're part of a team, and you're committed to the outcome but the others aren't.

That will suck energy out of you faster than a ten-mile run in one hundred–degree weather. A boss that only sees the things you do wrong is a big energy robber. Those situations are tougher, because you can't simply banish a coworker or a boss from your life. But you do have to make a decision about your long-term happiness. You're not going to have any if you're being sucked dry eight hours a day.

If you're doing your best to avoid energy-sucking activities, it's obvious that you need to find things that give your energy back exponentially, and make sure your schedule is sprinkled with those things.

My "balance place" is my barn. My kids and I built it ourselves, and it holds a lot of the things I really enjoy—my dogs, my horse, and my boat. If it had a flat screen television in it, I could move in and be pretty happy.

The week I'm writing this chapter, I've been in five different states covering four time zones, and I've given nine presentations. Add in the responsibilities that come with the radio show and writing this book and it's clear to me I'm out of balance.

So when I get home on Friday afternoon, I'm going to change my focus. I'm going to get back to my barn and work with my animals. I'll hang out with my kids, and Margaret and I will take the horse out. I won't be thinking about the people I'm going to speak to Monday afternoon, and I won't be thinking about this book. By Monday morning, I'll have my energy back, it will be time to go back to work, and I won't be thinking about my barn.

I spoke about my "balance place" last night in a presentation, and a guy in the second row yelled out that he didn't have a barn. That's kind of missing the point.

If you've got a Harley-Davidson motorcycle, it can be your barn. My friend Matt Rudy, who's writing this book with me, has a red 1966 Oldsmobile, and every week he takes that car out for an hour-long drive on the back roads of Connecticut, by himself. He comes back smelling like exhaust—and back in balance. It doesn't matter if it's a garden outside your house, the track over at the local high school, or a room in the basement where you work on a hobby. Those are all "barns."

We all have a barn. It's the place we love to be. Find that place for yourself, and protect your time there. You don't want to look back someday with regret because you didn't keep your priorities in order, because you didn't bring the energy you had for the sales call or the business deal back home to the people who are there for you every day.

I haven't met a single person who, late in life, has said, "I wish I could have spent less time doing the things I love to do, in my favorite place." Make the choices now that will put you in those good places for the rest of your life.

The Value of Perspective

A couple of weeks ago, I was coming back from a trip to Wisconsin at the end of a very hectic week. I had been in six different cities over five days, and I was more than ready to get home.

An old friend of mine who is the CFO of one of the largest companies in Dallas asked me to stop by on my way home from the airport to talk to his employees for an hour or so. It wasn't the best timing, but Margaret and the kids weren't home anyway, so I figured I could spare the time.

When I was pulling out of the airport parking lot, I got a call from another friend, who told me he had heard about a shooting at a college, and that it might have been at LSU. My son John goes to LSU, so I immediately called his cell number. I didn't get any answer, which isn't normal.

As I drove, I called his number again and again. My mind was racing at that point, and I wasn't sure what to do next. Finally, my phone rang, and it was John. He was okay. The shooting had happened at another school.

I pulled into the parking lot of the place where I was going to speak, and I put my head back on the headrest and closed my eyes for a minute. I was so, so thankful.

I pulled a folder out of my briefcase and walked in and gave my talk. When I came back out again, the window on my truck was bashed in. My briefcase and all my luggage from my trip was gone—stolen out of the truck.

I lost my laptop, my digital tape recorder, my cell phone—everything. All the work I had done from that week and all the pictures I had taken to show my wife when I got home were gone.

As you can imagine, I was pretty steamed. It was broad daylight, in a decent part of Dallas, and the lot had a full-time security guard. But then I thought about the shooting in Louisiana that could easily have been at LSU, where my son was—and how thankful I had been just a few hours ago that it hadn't been there.

I had lost a few things, but it didn't matter. I could get the "stuff" back. What was important was what I still had.

I'm sure there are parts of what I teach that might make you feel a little overwhelmed. I don't want to leave you with the idea that you need to make a blizzard of lists and commitments and promises for the rest of your life, and that if you fail just once you're a bad person. That's not it at all.

My greatest hope is to be able to help you see the things that are important in *your* life, and try to help you get some perspective on how to protect those things and on how to enjoy them more fully.

I'm a person who needs a lot of external organization. I need lists, charts, and folders, just to keep track of where I am day to day. It's just the set of tools I have. If somebody had come to me when I was twenty with the kind of strategies I've been describing in this book, I would have saved myself so much trouble and heartache. On the other hand, my wife is somebody who is internally organized. She keeps things in her head, and she doesn't need a system of lists and notes.

My goal isn't to come at you with some big, restrictive, difficult program that you have to follow religiously for the rest of your life. Frankly, for most people, that's a turnoff. There's a reason why the time frames in this book are forty-eight hours. It's a time frame that's perfect for trying something new and thinking about things in a different way.

Forty-Eight-Hour Action Plan

1. Commit to not leaving your office (or home) without writing down what you're going to do the next day. This does two things: it helps set your priorities and focus for the next day, and it provides separation. When you write the list, put it down and leave it to the next day with the security of knowing you don't have to remember or obsess over it. Your list will be waiting.

2. Make a list of the priorities in your life—in order—and place them where you can see them for the next two mornings. On the second day, write a number grade (on a scale of 1–10) next to each priority, summing up how well you're doing accomplishing it. Then, ask the person closest to you to take the same list and mark a grade for each of your priorities. When you compare numbers, I promise you'll see some surprises.

3. Don't forget to celebrate checking things off your to-do list. It's a lot of responsibility to hold yourself so accountable for what you do from day to day. When you do a great job following through, you set yourself apart in this world and build real balance between work and home. Make sure check-off time is a fun time of celebration.

Bringing It All Together

Do you know what I love the most about a brand-new day? You get to take what you learned yesterday and move it forward. And you get to let go of what you needed to let go of, so it won't slow you down.

I'm not a motivational speaker. That's not why I'm here. It's not why I make those three hundred trips a year to speak to companies and organizations. And it's not why I wrote this book.

"Motivation" is too limiting a word. Motivation is just getting you to do something faster. It doesn't even speak to whether or not you actually want to do it.

My goal for this book was to *inspire* you—inspire you to want the great things in life for yourself. And to help you figure out what those things are and how to go get them.

Organizations like Dell computer, Southwest Airlines, IBM, and the National Association of Home Builders form the framework of what I do every week. They're the ones that bring me in to speak to their people. But the truth is that the companies aren't what matters—you matter.

You make a difference. And if you've made it this far, to the last chapter of this book, you're a giver. You're somebody who wants to learn how to learn more, and how to give more. The angry people would never have gotten this far; the quitters wouldn't have, either.

You might find yourself stuck in a place where you're doing the same things day in, day out, but you know there's more out there. You know there's a better way to live your life—a way to be happier and more satisfied, and to give more back. And I give you so much credit for continuing to search for ways to get more out of your life. And I thank you for letting me be a part of that process.

The whole idea behind the forty-eight-hour framework we've been working on in each of these chapters is to help you channel all of the emotions that are a part of life in the same direction. In the direction of giving more back to the people around you. Because I believe that giving back to the people you love is the key to feeling happy and satisfied with life.

Some of you are probably thinking, "Is he trying to make me feel guilty for not doing more? For not giving back?"

That's absolutely not what I'm trying to do.

It's about finding the something that finally fulfills you—more than any "stuff" would.

What I'm asking you to do here is to look in the mirror and notice the positive things about yourself and your situation, the things that make you you. And when you look in that mirror, I want you to embrace the one idea that's been a common thread through this entire book.

Growth is good. You need to grow.

The world is changing around you. You're an important person in the lives of the people in your family and the people in your business. If you don't grow—and decide the direction of that growth—you're going to get pushed in a direction you might not have picked otherwise. And getting pushed like that makes you less able to help the people around you.

Are you going to be able to structure your life exactly according to plan? Absolutely not. Life is like white-water rafting—you can't control the river. But you need to have a plan for how to tackle it, so you can influence the outcome. Otherwise, you're going to get thrown into the rocks.

This might be the last chapter of this book, but I'm sure you know by now that I believe you're never done writing—and rewriting—the chapters of your life. And I believe that you'll get so much more happiness and satisfaction out of life if you don't wait for things to happen to you that will demand that you change.

My youngest child is going off to college this year. Margaret and I are going to have an empty house for the first time in a long time. It's a bittersweet time for us—we're so proud that our kids have grown up to be strong, independent, loving adults, but we're obviously going to miss having them here. We're not going to plunge into a depression in the fall, when Zach leaves for LSU. We've already made plans to downsize our house and move closer to the city, so we can do some fun things together—things that weren't a priority when we had kids at home. For years, I've said no to companies that wanted me to travel abroad because it would take me away from home for too many nights. Now, we'll be able to travel together to places we've always wanted to go and have some great new experiences.

When you start embracing the idea of change—and decide that you're going to choose the direction of those changes—you become alive again. You're not living to avoid fear or pain.

So many people stop growing and changing in life, and it isn't for the reasons you might think. It doesn't have anything to do with being disappointed about losing out on a promotion, losing money, or even having your heart broken. We've all seen plenty of famous people look like they "had it all," at least in terms of what would make the average person jealous. Who wouldn't want to have millions of dollars, expensive cars and jets, and enough clothes to fill an entire floor of a house? But many of those people who have it all—money, fame, "stuff"—end up depressed, addicted to something, or just plain broken.

What they don't have—and what anybody who is feeling unfulfilled doesn't have—is the basic human necessity of appreciation. It works two ways. If you're appreciative of what you have and you feel as though the people around you appreciate you for who you are—not what you own or what you do—then you can truly be satisfied.

That's just as true for an NBA player or the CEO of a Fortune 500 company as it is for an average person like me or like you.

When you feel that appreciation in your life, and you learn to give back, you see that the appreciation and support comes your way as well. You truly understand that you're significant to the people who love you, and you can accept everything this world has to offer.

If you aren't looking for ways to grow and change in your life, it's very easy to switch on a sort of autopilot. Your days don't have meaning, and you start losing the ability to look forward to the things ahead.

That's a hollow feeling, and I've seen it in some of my closest friends. They could eat a $500 meal every night of the week and finish off two $300 bottles of wine on top of it, then jump into a $150,000 sports car to drive to their million-dollar home. But it's never enough. It doesn't satisfy them.

In the last eight chapters, you've heard me say more than once that average people appreciate what they have only after they lose it, while good people appreciate what they have while they have it. That's the point I'm trying to hammer home again here.

It's why I asked you to look in the mirror and see the positive things, because once you do that, you can start to feel grateful for what you already have, and find the sliver of hope that will fuel you to resolve the problems in your life.

The Five "Why" Questions for The Good Life

Day to day, you might feel like it's a struggle to keep seeing the "why" instead of just the "how." The answers to these five "why" questions will help you see how important the "why" is, and what's at stake:

Why Is Enthusiasm Important?

Real enthusiasm isn't something you put on or take off like a shirt. You can't just flip the switch and be "on." I was doing my radio show the other day, and I saw a name on the call screen that I knew very well—Brian from Colorado Springs. He's been one of my best friends since we were nine, and he started his call with a joke. "If you're wondering if Bryan's like this almost all the time, the answer is yes," he said. "When he's rolling, we can't get a word in."

He was talking about my excitement for life, and the energy I put into the programs I do. It doesn't matter if it's on the show, in this book, or in my living room, I'm the same guy. Notice he didn't say *all* the time. It's how you live your life *most* of the time that defines you. We all have off days, where we struggle to find the energy we know we're going to need. The key is to be enthusiastic and optimistic with your thoughts, as consistently as you can. It's a habit like any other.

My friend Mark Marvel is the president of the Blind Ambitions Group (blindambitionsgroups.org), which promotes job opportunities for people who have lost their vision. Mark lost his sight almost ten years ago from diabetes, and if that wasn't challenging enough, he's also had his foot amputated because of the disease. But Mark is probably the most enthusiastic, positive person I know. When I was thinking about this chapter, I called him to ask him how he did it.

"Life is how you choose to live it," he said. "I could be bitter about losing my sight, or I can embrace the life I still have and enjoy it. If I get enthusiastic about something I am doing, the people around me start getting into the activity I am doing and stop thinking about things like 'That poor guy is blind and has an amputated foot.'"

Mark told me that enthusiasm attracts others who are enthusiastic, and for him it's a simple matter of wanting to be around positive, happy people. Energy breeds energy. He's also secure in his faith, and content to know that if something does happen to him, he's going to a good place.

I don't want you to think you have to be bouncing off the walls and talking nonstop to show your enthusiasm. Show it your way. You might be a more quiet, reflective person. Your enthusiasm could come across more as warmth and reassurance for those around you. That's okay. It's never going to work unless you're being you.

Why Do You Need Your Emotions to Work for You and Not Against You?

Learning how to manage your emotions is a critical part of surviving company and family life. It doesn't mean you stop feeling or stop caring. It means understanding what's happening to you and why you're reacting the way you are. Instead of making your decisions based on emotion, then backing them up by trying to find logic that fits, your goal should be to flip those two things around. Make the decisions based on logic, and let the emotions work as motivation for the decision.

If you do let your emotions get the better of you, you're usually going to struggle—whether it's in a work situation, a family argument, or in the arena as a bull rider, like I was for many years. When I was riding, if you fell off the bull, you got hurt the worst if you panicked and lost control of your emotions. Depending on how you fell off (or got thrown), you could avoid getting hurt if you kept your composure and didn't panic. If you let your emotions get the better of you, it hurt your reflexes, and you could be in serious danger.

It's one thing to understand that you need to control your emotions. But how do you actually do it?

The first step is to stop pretending you're good at understanding and controlling your emotions if you aren't. I know I'm not. I struggle with focus, and staying on track, so I know I have to work on it every day. I do it using step-by-step processes. My kids had the ability to throw me off track right away, like asking me why avoiding smoking was such a big deal. So I decided that when I started to feel angry or ready to give a lecture, I'd count to ten before I said a word. It gave me the time for my brain to catch up to my emotions.

Another strategy is to ask for a second opinion from a person you trust. If you're in an emotionally charged situation, it could be as simple as a quick e-mail to a friend or mentor that says "Here's what I'm thinking about this situation I'm in. Am I seeing all the sides of this problem?" You're not looking for somebody to make your decisions for you or resolve your problems. You're just getting confirmation on your judgment—and more important, giving yourself time to take a breath and consider your course of action before doing something rash. Remember, if you're not in a hurry, don't act like you are.

When you get a handle on your emotions, what you develop is perspective. You start to see the real relationships between things, and you understand what things are important and what things aren't. You'll stop jeopardizing the things that are important by reacting badly to things that aren't important.

Why Do You Need to Understand and Control Worry?

Most people fall into one of two categories when it comes to worrying. Some are compulsive worriers, who get stressed out about details large and small and are frightened and anxious about making decisions. Others go the other way and decide that they're just going to deny things that deserve worry or attention. They're the people who just seem to be resigned to whatever happens to them, good or bad.

Worry is something you're going to have to face in your life, whether you want to or not. My wife likes to say that worry comes from fear, and fear is life's message to you that you need to pay attention. In other words, paying attention to legitimate worries and fears can save you from pain and disaster.

Worry can be your best friend if you recognize the legitimate concerns that brought it on, act on them, and then let the worry go. The problems start when you either don't let the worry go, or you refuse to recognize the concerns that need to be addressed.

What things are causing you stress right now? Pick a situation about which you're really dreading the outcome. Maybe it's a job review with a boss you don't love, your child's behavior problem, or an audit from the IRS. To confront your worry, start by visualizing the most undesirable outcome. Maybe you'll get fired. Maybe you'll have to go down and meet with the principal of the school. Maybe you'll have to write a big check. By visualizing the worst-case scenario, you've immediately turned something nebulous and speculative into something concrete. You can focus your attention on a single outcome—not twenty different ones—and say to yourself, "What steps do I need to put in place to avoid this outcome?" I bet you'll also start realizing that most of the time, even the worst case isn't an insurmountable tragedy.

Most of the time, the things that worry you won't be nearly as bad as you thought, and by being prepared for the worst-case scenario, you're going to be pleasantly surprised.

Last year, a man approached me after I finished a big speaking engagement, and he asked me if I ever got nervous in front of a big crowd.

"I sure hope so," I said, without a hint of sarcasm. "Because the day I don't worry about what I do is the day I quit doing this. It means I don't care about the outcome."

In the short term, when you're getting a project in shape at work or you're dealing with a crisis at home, worry is useful. It pushes you hard to do what you need to do to solve the problem.

If you can look at yourself and know that you've done all you can to prepare and you've given your best effort, that's when you can let go of the worry and accept whatever consequences there are. After all, what more can you do than all you can do?

Why Is It Important to Decide What's Important?

It's certainly human nature to take the path of least resistance. We're wired to look for the simplest ways to solve problems. Unfortunately, the simplest ways aren't always the most satisfying ways—or the ones that work the best for the long term.

Let me use a simple school yard example. When you're five years old and you see another child with a toy you really want, the simplest way to get it would be to go over and snatch it away from that kid. That's something we all did when we were little. And, of course, Mom gave us a stern talking-to about why that wasn't acceptable behavior.

Life doesn't change that much from the school yard. It's just a matter of degree. You can certainly live your life just grabbing for what you want and not caring about how the people around you respond. You're also going to live that life alone—and unsatisfied. If you accept the idea that life is a compromise with the people who are important to you, then you have to come up with a way to prioritize the way you spend your time.

By deciding what's important in *your* life, you're creating a set of rules for yourself and your family. Those rules will help you determine when it makes sense to push and sacrifice for something, and when it's better to find a simpler, easier way.

We've talked a lot about setting goals and making no lists, and all of these philosophies certainly fit together. My family is my priority, so I base my decisions on what speaking engagements to take on how long I'm going to have to be away from home. When my kids are all out of the house next year, I'll be able to change my schedule if I like, because I can make trips with my wife and not worry about leaving the kids home.

Not all of the decisions you make are going to be black and white. So many things in life are much easier than they used to be. If you don't want to do housework, you can hire someone to come and do it for you. If you want to be in touch with your office twenty-four hours a day, with technology you can be. If you don't feel like standing in front of the stove for two hours, you can call and order a pizza.

But, like I said, the simplest solution isn't always the most satisfying one. Some people might decide that spending time with the kids is important, so they don't want to waste time in the kitchen when they get home from work. Ordering a pizza seems like the best choice in terms of time management, but is it the best choice when it comes to setting an example for the kids?

When I was growing up, my dad demanded that my brother and sister and I complete a wide variety of chores and jobs around the house—from cleaning up to fixing fences. Part of it was a parental power struggle: he wanted to make sure we knew who was in charge. But I didn't understand the bigger picture until later. He wanted to make sure we knew how to do a variety of basic jobs, so that we could solve more problems on our own later in life. It didn't mean that for the rest of our lives we should feel obligated to do all the hard labor ourselves. It makes sense to outsource jobs you don't want to do anymore. But knowing *how* to do things is important.

Those are the lessons that stay with a person for life. A couple of Texas summers ago, my boys and I put a new roof on our barn. Now, we're talking about a big barn. On the second day of work, I looked over to my boys, who were sweating in the hundred-degree heat, and I asked them if they liked doing this.

"Yes," they said. "It's a family project."

Then I asked if they'd like doing it as a job.

"Heck no."

After the roofing experience, every time the kids brought home a report card and the grades were awesome (which was often), I'd ask them what inspired them to do so well. "Putting the roof on the barn," they'd say, with a laugh.

I believe life should be a mix of the satisfying and the convenient. You don't have to go out and pave your own driveway. But you'll be more satisfied with the garden in the backyard if you learn about plants and vegetables on the Internet with your kids, then go out and plant it together.

If you know how to persevere and accomplish things when the road is difficult—and you understand when it's worth it to let something go so you can do things that are more important to you and your family—you really understand The Good Life Rules.

I heard my friend Jim Rohn, the great business development leader, speak at a conference my company produced in Toronto more than twenty years ago. The message from his talk still sticks with me today. If you do things that are easy for other people *not* to do, you're going to stand out—either as an employee or an organization. I believe that's 100 percent true. But it's not the only piece of the puzzle. Doing things the hard way just for the sake of doing them that way is a dead end. I know a lot of people who believe that hard work is its own reward. I'm not going to say hard work isn't a virtue. It absolutely is. But mindless hard work just keeps you from your family and friends. Spending ten hours fixing something that could have been fixed in four—and missing the soccer game or the pictures before the prom—is just stubborn pride and getting stuck on an idea that time has passed by. I believe that people often "keep busy" because the work is something familiar. If they stopped the busy work, they'd have to learn how to deal with a different kind of situation.

Why Do You Need to Find Something That Inspires You?

Before I became a speaker myself, I owned a company that put together speaking engagements for other companies and organizations. For more than twenty-five years, I've been up close and personal with virtually every person in the "motivational" business. I've heard them speak. I've read all the books. Is there some bad information out there? Absolutely.

But there's also some great, great stuff. The common thread in messages that really resonate with people—and the ones that really work—is that you can't make a dramatic, long-term change in your life if you aren't inspired to do so.

Willpower by itself won't work. Fear might work, but only for a short time. You need to be inspired to change. If nothing moves you, then nothing is *going* to move you. If nothing matters to you, then nothing is going to be important enough to you to want to sacrifice and work to change.

You need to have the ability to dream at the highest of levels—to be inspired by a goal—to have the energy it takes to live The Good Life. When you understand exactly why you're meant to do something—not how to do it, but *why*—it will change you. I call it the "clearing of the eyes." I'll be speaking to a large group, and we'll be talking about the same things we've been covering in the last eight chapters, and all of a sudden the eyes of the crowd change. They go from troubled and cloudy to bright and clear. It's the look of people who have a purpose.

How do you get that purpose? First, you have to understand just how much of your life is going to be devoted to work. Whether you like it or hate it, you're going to be spending more than half your waking hours every week at your job. If you don't decide for yourself what your priorities are—what makes you happy—you stand a high risk of getting trapped in a job you hate. Now, if that job pays a ton of money, and the money gives you flexibility to spend the rest of your time doing something you love, like hanging out with your family, volunteering on the weekends, or racing vintage motorcycles, that's a choice you can make. But it needs to be a *choice*.

Too many people end up in default jobs and default careers because they've essentially been herded that way over months and years. Don't be one of those people. There's always time to take more control over where you're headed professionally. Life is too short not to be happy, and too long not to do well.

When it comes to family and the other people who are most important to you in life, you've got the ultimate source of inspiration. I can tell you that nothing is better than having a relationship with someone—a wife, a child, a brother or sister, a friend—who knows you, loves you, and is there to support you unconditionally. Protecting and growing those relationships is what drives me every single day.

My wife and I have been married thirty years, and I can't imagine anything better than growing old with her. We've had hard times and great times, and there's nothing better than knowing you've got somebody at your side who has been through the same things you have, and who knows you better than anybody. Somebody who loves you because of who you are, not what you do or the things you have. We have three great kids, and the moment I held each one of them for the first time, I knew that I could never walk away.

There are no guarantees in life. I've heard people say that they're scared to build a connection to people that way, because it would be so painful to lose a spouse, a child—or even a parent. Could it be terribly painful and break your heart? Yes.

But the real connections we make in life are so worth it. These connections give you the inspiration to get up and do it every day—even when you're tired and it's hard.

They make The Good Life.

Epilogue

There's no better way to end this book not by what I say but with what my father says about me:

You would expect a father to be proud of his son, especially when he's accomplished as much as my son Bryan has. And I'm certainly proud of Bryan's role in helping so many people, families, and organizations find that better balance between work and home so many of us need to be as happy and productive as we can be. I own every one of his DVDs and CDs—and not just because I'm his dad. I gave a few copies of his first audio presentation to some of the people at my company, Progress Rail, for a sales meeting. The material was so popular, I ended up buying more than five hundred copies for employees across the country to use for sales training.

I'm also proud that the caring and enthusiasm that radiates from these pages is absolutely genuine Bryan. The man you see here is the man who has been my best buddy for fifty years—there's nobody in the world I'd rather hunt, fish, or ride with, and we've filled a lifetime with great memories. The way he's raised his family—and the love he shows to the important people in his life—is proof that he walks the walk.

And it hasn't always been an easy walk, either.

Bryan has always had the energy and enthusiasm he shows today. More than once, we headed out to fish, and by the time I got to the spot from the car, he had caught his limit and mine too! It's always been impossible for him to sit still for more than a minute.

But as a young person, he could not get up in front of people and speak. He didn't do much reading, and none of his high school teachers could seem to draw him out. He's been at the bottom, and he knows what it's like to have a problem. But he wouldn't let that shyness destroy or deprive him of The Good Life he describes so well here. He fought and struggled to get better, and he worked to reveal the gift that's always been within him. It's such a treat to see him get up in front of people and make a difference—and know the journey he's taken to get to where he is. He's the same Bryan we've always known, but it's amazing to think of how different he is from the shy little kid who wouldn't come out when guests came to the house.

So many people are vocal about their beliefs when it's easy, but when it comes time to do something truly unselfishly, they fall short. I know I have. It's tempting to say you're too busy, and it's easy to let the things that are really important slip.

Bryan's optimistic outlook and enthusiasm for life have always been contagious for me, and I know it will be for you, too.

Dick Dodge
Colorado Springs, Colo.
April 2008

Appendix

The Forty-Five Undeniable Truths of Life

I've been sharing The Good Life Rules—in various forms—to groups for more than twenty years. Over that time, I've been compiling and editing the list of what I call the Forty-Five Undeniable Truths of Life. These are the truths I've used to build The Good Life Rules, because they've held so true in all the personal and professional challenges I've experienced, as well as in the stories told to me by people across the country.

1. Love. What you feel in your heart you must act on. It is the window of truth.

2. Diminishing Intent. What you don't act on within a forty-eight-hour window, you will lose.

3. Habits/Control. You feel positive about yourself to the extent that you feel in control. Values/Principles plus Actions will determine whether or not you are in control. If you're working against this formula, you will create stress.

4. Responsibility. You must take full responsibility for your actions.

5. Compensation. Whatever you put in, you will get out. The more value you bring to your time, the more time will pay you for your value.

6. Value. Your rewards in life will be in direct proportion to the level of service or value that you offer in life.

7. Applied Effort. All things are amenable to hard work. Balance is the key.

8. Overcompensation. Always put in more than you take out.

9. Preparation. Professionals always take more time to prepare than others do.

10. Action. The more you take on, the more efficient you become.

11. Making a Choice. Nothing really happens until you make a choice. Right or wrong is better than no choice at all.

12. Imagination. It is your imagination that creates your opportunity.

13. Open Mind. Be clear on your goal, but be flexible on how you might attain it.

14. Concentration. The ability to stay on a task until completed. When you are where you are, be there.

15. Rest. You must have rest. Just don't rest too long.

16. Belief. If you don't believe, why would they?

17. Change. Disgust and resolve are two of the great mental attitudes that lead to change.

18. Asking. Asking is the beginning of receiving.

19. Basics. Success is neither magical nor mysterious. Success is the natural consequence of consistently applying fundamentals.

20. Persuasion. Better to understate than to overstate. Let people be surprised that you delivered more than you promised.

21. Discipline. The lack of discipline starts to crowd our self-esteem. Discipline has within it the potential for creating future miracles.

22. Learning. When somebody is traveling down the wrong road, they don't need motivation to speed them up. They need education to turn them around.

23. Caring. Show your contempt for the problem and your concern for the person. The more you care, the stronger you can be.

24. Emotions. Emotions will either guide you toward the goal or lead you away from it.

25. Experience. Take time to remember the past so that you will be able to draw from your experiences. This will allow you to reinvest in the future for a different and better outcome.

26. Fascination. Fascination is one step beyond interest. Interested people want to see it work; fascinated people want to know how it works. Develop a childlike fascination with life and people.

27. Fear. If you do what you fear the most, then you control fear.

28. Sharing. Giving is better than receiving because giving starts the receiving process.

29. Goals. We all have goals whether or not we set them. If you set your goals, they are your standards that you have set for yourself. If you haven't set them, somebody else will set them for you. I'll bet they don't set them as high as you would have. The ultimate reason for setting goals is so that you become the person you need to be to achieve them.

30. Wealth. The philosophy of the rich versus the poor is the rich invest their money and spend what is left. The poor spend their money and invest what is left.

31. Happiness. Happiness is not an accident nor is it something you wish for. Happiness is something you design in your life. It is a choice. Happiness is not something you postpone for the future; it is something you design for the present.

32. Health. Make sure that your outside is a good reflection of your inside.

33. Ignorance. What you don't know will hurt you.

34. Association. You must constantly ask yourself these questions:

- Who am I around?
- What are they doing to me?
- What have they got me reading?
- What have they got me saying?
- Where do they have me going?
- What do they have me thinking?
- What do they have me becoming?
- Then ask yourself, "Is this okay?"

35. Leadership. The challenge of leadership is to be strong but not rude; kind but not weak; bold but not a bully; thoughtful but not lazy; humble but not timid; proud but not arrogant. Keep humor as a key.

36. Lifestyle. You must design your own lifestyle. Great lifestyles happen because the person planned it that way.

37. Neglect. One of the reasons many people don't have what they want is neglect. Neglect starts out as an infection, then becomes a disease.

38. Parenting. There is no greater leadership challenge than parenting.

39. Personal Development. Income seldom exceeds personal development.

40. Halo Effect. Each individual must be committed to maintaining the reputation of all. And everyone must be committed to maintaining the reputation of each individual.

41. Results. Results is the name of the game.

42. Sophistication. Most people are just trying to get through the day. Sophisticated people are trying to get from the day.

43. Vocabulary. Vocabulary enables us to interpret and to express. If you have a limited vocabulary, you will also have a limited vision and a limited future.

44. Fighting. You must keep fighting if you want to survive. Health, happiness, and success depend upon the fighting spirit of each person. The big thing is not what happens to us in life, but what we do about it.

45. Desire. Desire creates achievers and inspires them to greatness.

My Goals List

Live a why-focused life
Read the Bible daily
Get up 30 minutes earlier than usual
Work out four times week
Finish the barn
Finish the new program
Work on new website
Complete Talent DNA
Start selling my house
Bring energy home
Forgive, let go, laugh, enjoy life
Be there for my family

My No List

The no list is sometimes more important than the goal list. It is hard to add on good goals in your life unless you subtract. You have only so much time in a day. And the best way to subtract is to make an "I will not do this any more" list, called a no list. This will then give you the time to do the things that matter most in life.

Will not travel or speak on Sunday

Will not service my lawn (that's sad)

Will not allow ungodly things in my life

Will not use the word *can't*

Will not leave work without a game plan for next day

Will no longer put off until tomorrow what can be done today

Will no longer let my busy life take away from my ability to have time to think

Will no longer be disorganized

Will not fall into behavior patterns that lead to addictive behavior

Will no longer be afraid to say NO

Will not be who I am not

Will no longer be afraid to tell people the truth

Will not ignore talking about things that I don't want to talk about

Will not give up family time for the sake of work (paid or unpaid)

Will no longer say no to the things I'm afraid of

Recommended Reading

My Favorites

The Holy Bible
Tuesdays with Morrie by Mitch Albom
Think and Grow Rich by Napoleon Hill
Who Moved My Cheese? by Spencer Johnson, M.D.
The Richest Man in Babylon by George S. Clason
The 21 Irrefutable Laws of Leadership by John C. Maxwell
High Five! The Magic of Working Together by Ken Blanchard,
  Sheldon Bowles, Don Carew, and Eunice Parisi-Carew
Becoming the Obvious Choice by Bryan Dodge and David Cottrell
How to Win Friends and Influence People by Dale Carnegie
Monday Morning Leadership by David Cottrell

*Why Buy In? The Survival Primer for Free Thinkers in the
Stereotypical Business World* by T. B. Fisher

*The Richest Man Who Ever Lived: King Solomon's Secrets to Success,
Wealth, and Happiness* by Steven K. Scott

Recommendations from Friends

Jack Grehan recommends *Lists to Live By*, compiled by Alice
Gray, Steve Stephens, and John Van Diest

Matthew Carter recommends *Financial Peace* by Dave Ramsey

Donna McCright recommends *How to Get into the Bible* by
Stephen M. Miller and *Fish! A Remarkable Way to Boost
Morale and Improve Results* by Stephen C. Lundin, Harry
Paul, and John Christensen

Margaret Dodge recommends *The Birth Order Book: Why We Are
The Way We Are* by Dr. Kevin Leman

Amity Albee Carriere recommends *The Power of Now: A Guide to
Spiritual Enlightenment* by Eckhart Tolle

Lori Puckett recommends *Results Project's Excalibur: Answers for
Parents with ADD/ADhD Concerns* by Steve V. Plog, M.D.

John Hoehl recommends *Alexander the Great's Art of Strategy* by
Partha Bose

Otto Katt, III, recommends *How I Raised Myself From Failure to
Success in Selling* by Frank Bettger

Pam Anderson recommends *Back to Basics for Finding Sanity in
an Insane World!* by Bob Anderson, Ph.D.

Bryan Parkhurst recommends *The Four Agreements: A Practical
Guide to Personal Freedom* by Don Miguel Ruiz

Kim Best recommends *Standing for Something* by Gordon B.
Hinckley

Recommendations for Physical Health and Fitness

Fit or Fat by Covert Bailey
Fit for Life by Harvey and Marilyn Diamond
Medical Makeover: The Revolutionary No-Willpower Program for Lifetime Health by Robert M. Giller, M.D., and Kathy Mathews
The Mollen Method by Dr. Art Mollen

Recommendations for Emotional Health

Who Moved My Cheese? by Spencer Johnson, M.D.
Ninety Days to Financial Fitness by Joan German-Grapes
The Magic of Thinking Big by David Schwartz, Ph.D.
J.K. Lasser's Personal Investment Annual by Judith Headington McGee and Jerrold Dickson
The Only Investment Guide You Will Ever Need by Andrew Tobias
The Magic and Power of Self Image Psychology by Maxwell Maltz
How to Get More for Your Money by Sylvia Porter
Touch the Top of the World by Erik Weihenmayer
Wealth: How to Get It, How to Keep It by Herb D. Vest and Lynn R. Niedermeier

Recommendations for Books on ADD and ADHD

Healing ADD: The Breakthrough Program That Allows You to See and Heal the 6 Types of ADD by Daniel G. Amen, M.D.
Results Project's Excalibur: Answers for Parents with ADD/ADhD Concerns by Steve V. Plog, M.D.

Recommendations for Books on Attitude and Balanced Living

Beware of Naked Man Who Offers You His Shirt by
    Harvey MacKay
Man's Search for Meaning by Viktor E. Frankl
Lifebalance by Richard and Linda Eyre
Your Erroneous Zone by Wayne Dyer
Napkin Notes: On the Art of Living by G. Michael Durst, Ph.D.
First Things First by Stephen R. Covey
The 7 Habits of Highly Effective People by Stephen R. Covey
Principle-Centered Leadership by Stephen R. Covey
How to Win Friends and Influence People by Dale Carnegie
*Professional Presence: The Total Program for Gaining That Extra
    Edge in Business by America's Top Corporate Image Consultant* by
    Susan Bixler
Seeds of Greatness by Denis Waitley
The Man in the Mirror by Patrick Morley
In My Own Words by Mother Teresa
The Road to Happiness Is Full of Potholes by Tim Connor

Recommendations for Books on Management and Leadership

Negotiating Rationally by Max H. Bazerman
Excelerate: Growing in the New Economy by Nuala Beck
Shifting Gears Thriving in the New Economy by Nuala Beck
On Becoming a Leader by Warren Bennis
Technotrends by Daniel Burrus
Sales Manager's Desk Book by Gene Garofalo
The Goal by Eliyahu M. Goldratt

The Executive Odyssey by Frederick G. Harmon

Secrets of the Master Sale Managers by Porter Henry

A Passion for Excellence by Tom Peters and Nancy Austin

Compensating Your Sales Force by W. G. Ryckman and
    Robert G. Head

Delegate: The Key to Successful Management by Harold Taylor

The Founding Fathers on Leadership by Donald T. Phillips

Alexander the Great's Art of Strategy by Partha Bose

Monday Morning Leadership by David Cottrell

Monday Morning Leadership for Women by Valerie Sokolosky

The Leadership Secrets of Santa Claus by Eric Harvey,
    David Cottrell, and Al Lucia

The Manager's Coaching Handbook by David Cottrell and
    Mark Layton

The Manager's Communication Handbook by David Cottrell and
    Eric Harvey

Management Insights by Ken Carnes, David Cottrell, and
    Mark C. Layton

Listen Up, Leader! by David Cottrell

Leadership . . . Biblically Speaking by David Cottrell

136 Effective Presentation Tips by Tony Jeary and David Cottrell

175 Ways to Get More Done in Less Time by David Cottrell and
    Mark C. Layton

180 Ways to Walk the Leadership Talk by John Baldoni

180 Ways to Walk the Recognition Talk by Eric Harvey

Becoming the Obvious Choice by Bryan Dodge and David Cottrell

Ethics 4 Everyone by Eric Harvey and Scott Airitam

Nuts 'n Bolts Leadership by Eric Harvey and Paul Sims

Sticking to It: The Art of Adherence by Lee J. Colan

Walk the Talk . . . and Get the Results You Want by Eric Harvey
    and Al Lucia

I Wish You Would Just . . . by Todd McDonald and
    Kyndra Wilson

Recommendations for Books on the Spiritual and Relationships

Seven Promises of a Promise Keeper by Bill Bright
Transferable Concepts for a Powerful Living by Bill Bright
Love for a Lifetime by James C. Dobson
More Than a Carpenter by Josh McDowell
Effective Prayer Life by Chuck Smith
How to Get Control of Your Time and Your Life by Alan Lakein
Personal Organization by Harold Tyler
The Organized Executive by Stephanie Winston
Celebration of Discipline by Richard J. Foster

Recommendations for Books on Selling

Swim with the Sharks Without Being Eaten Alive by
   Harvey MacKay
World Class Selling by Art Mortell
7 Strategies for Wealth and Happiness by Jim Rohn
How to Master the Art of Selling by Tom Hopkins
Power Talking by George R. Walther
Secrets of Closing the Sale by Zig Ziglar
See You at the Top by Zig Ziglar
The First Time Sales Manager by Theodore Tyssen
Influence: The Psychology of Persuasion by Robert B. Cialdini
Marketing Your Product by Donald G. Cyr and Douglas Gray
The Revolution in Sales and Marketing by Allan J. Magrath
The Ultimate Marketing Tool by Edward L. Nash
Positioning: The Battle for Your Mind by Al Ries and Jack Trout
The Greatest Miracle in the World by Og Mandino
The Sale by Don Hutson

Recommendations for Books on Selling Real Estate

How to Master the Art of Listing Real Estate by Tom Hopkins
How to List and Sell Real Estate by Danielle Kennedy
Why They Buy by Robert B. Settle and Pamela L. Alreck
Megatrends by John Naisbitt
Preparing for the Twenty-First Century by Paul Kennedy
Marketing Your Service Business by Jean Withers and
    Carol Vipperman
Managing the Obvious by Charles Coonradt
Time Management for Entrepreneurs by Dan Kennedy

Recommendations for Books on Sales Management

One Minute Manager by Kenneth Blanchard and
    Spencer Johnson
The A to Z of Sales Management by John Fenton
The New Sales Manager's Survival Guide by David Arthur Stumm
Successful Strategies for Sales Managers by Floyd Wickman
Do's and Taboos Around the World by Rodger E. Axtell
Secrets of Power Presentations by Peter Urs Bender
Firing on All Cylinders by Jim Clemmer
The Secrets of Super Selling by Lynea Corson
How to Get the Most Out of Sales Meetings by James Dance
What They Don't Teach You in Sales 101 by Steven Drozdeck
The Instant Millionaire by Mark Fisher
Relationship Selling by Karen Johnston
Sales Success by Dan Kennedy
Winning Strategies in Selling by Jack Kinder, Jr.
Salesmanship and Business Efficiency by James Samuel Knox

Professional Selling by David Kurtz
The Greatest Salesman in the World by Og Mandino
Strategic Selling by Robert B. Miller and Stephen E. Heiman
Successful Large Account Management by Robert B. Miller and
    Stephen E. Heiman
Live for Success by John T. Molloy
Negotiating the Big Sale by Gerard I. Nierenberg
Major Account Sales Strategy by Neil Rackham
Managing Major Sales by Neil Rackham
Horse Sense by Al Ries and Jack Trout
Awaken the Giant Within by Anthony Robbins
Making Time to Sell by Harold L. Taylor
No Bull Selling by Hank Trisler
The New Psychology of Persuasion and Motivation in Selling by
    Robert A. Whitney
Stop Selling, Start Partnering by Larry Wilson
Changing the Game by Larry Wilson
Building Customer Loyalty by JoAnna Brandi
Listen Up! Customer Service by David Cottrell and
    Mark C. Layton
180 Ways to Walk the Customer Service Talk by Eric Harvey
The Psychology of Selling by Brian Tracy
24 Techniques for Closing the Sale by Brian Tracy

Recommendations for Books on Continuing Education and Personal Development

See You at the Top by Zig Ziglar
Goals by Zig Ziglar
Sell Your Way to the Top by Zig Ziglar
You Are a Natural Champion by Zig Ziglar
Success and the Self-Image by Zig Ziglar

How to be a Winner by Zig Ziglar
How to Master the Art of Selling by Tom Hopkins
Dig Your Well Before You're Thirsty by Harvey MacKay
The Secrets of Savvy Networking by Susan RoAne
What Do I Say Next? by Susan RoAne
How to Read a Person Like a Book by Gerard I. Nierenberg
The Art of Negotiation by Gerard I. Nierenberg
Success Is a Choice by Rick Pitino
Simple Steps to Impossible Dreams by Steven K. Scott
Goal Setting for Results by Gary Ryan Blair
You Gotta Get in the Game: Playing to Win in Business, Sales and Life by Billy Cox
The Dream Book by Billy Cox

Recommendation for Book on Business

Competency-Based Resumes: How to Bring Your Resume to the Top of the Pile by Robin Kessler and Linda A. Strasburg

Recommendations for Books on Finding Your Purpose

Life by Design by Todd Duncan
The Ultimate Gift by Jim Stovall
The On-Purpose Person (Making Your Life Make Sense) by Kevin W. McCarthy
Life is Not a Game of Perfect by Dr. Bob Rotella
The Purpose-Driven Life by Rick Warren
101 Secret Ways to Tell if You Are Living Your Life Purpose by Daniel Ortiz
What Should I Do With My Life? by Po Bronson

Index

Action, making decisions for, 64–66

Action plans. *See* Forty-eight-hour action plans

Addictions. *See also* Habits
picking replacements for, 19
pleasure and, 89
social component, 89

Argue component, of EAT plan, 44–47

Arrogance, Why Trap and, 41–42

Assessments, getting honest, 19

Bad habits. *See also* Habits
defining your, 91–94
sources of, 89–90

Balance. *See* Home-work balance

Balance place, protecting your, 143–45

"Barns," for balance places, 143–45

Blame, ownership of leadership and, 115–16

Blind Ambitions Group, 154

Books, learning and, 22–25. *See also* Reading

Careers, learning for new,
        25–27
Change
    celebrating, 18
    committing to, 16
    deciding what's important
        for, 5–7
    evaluating your
        surroundings for,
        13–16
    forty-eight-hour action
        plan for, 19
    getting into the game for,
        7–11
    looking up and, 11–13
    six steps to successful,
        16–18
    willingness to, 3, 4–5
Channell, Ken, 120
Choosing to be faithful
        rule, 3
Commitment
    lists for, 84
    showing, 84
Complacency, Why Trap
        and, 41
Concentration, great leaders
        and, 129
Cottrell, David, 115
Courage, great leaders and,
        128–29
Creating new habits rule, 3

Dedication, great leaders
        and, 128
Diminishing intent rule, 3
    defined, 53–54
    Kate's story, 55–56

Distraction, Why Trap and,
        41
Dodge, Bryan, 163–64
    Talent DNA assessment
        results for, 121–26
Dodge, Dick (father),
        163–64

Eager component, of EAT
        plan, 42–44
Easy times, faithfulness and,
        72–76
EAT plan, 3
    Argue component of,
        44–47
    Eager component of,
        42–44
    Thankfulness component
        of, 47–51
Emotions
    strategies for controlling,
        155–56
    working for you, not
        against you,
        154–56
Enthusiasm, importance of,
        153–54

Faith, The Good Life and,
        10
Faithfulness, 69–72
    easy times vs. hard times
        and, 72–76
    lists for, 84
    secret to, 76–79
Fallacy of Scheduling,
        134–36
Fear, Why Trap and, 42

Five "why" questions,
  for The Good Life,
  153–62
  Why do you need
    emotions working for
    you not against you?,
    154–56
  Why do you need to
    find something that
    inspires you?, 160–62
  Why do you need to
    understand and
    control worry?,
    156–57
  Why is enthusiasm
    important?, 153–54
  Why is it important
    to decide what's
    important?, 157–60
Focus, dialing in your, for
  home-work balance,
  141–42
Forty-eight-hour action
  plans
  for change, 19
  for faithfulness, 84–85
  for following your heart,
    66–67
  for goal setting, 102–3
  for home-work balance,
    147
  for leaders, 130–31
  for learning, 34–35
  for why in life, 51–52
Forty-eight-hour resolutions,
  56–58
  commitment to following
    your heart to, 58–62

Getting to why in life rule,
  3, 37–39
Getting to why rule, 3
Goal lists, priority lists vs.,
  140
Goal setting
  forty-eight-hour action
    plan for, 102–3
  making habit of,
    97–102
Good habits. *See also* Habits
  defining your, 91–94
  sources of, 89–90
Good Life, The
  components of, 57
  faith and, 10
  five "why" questions for,
    153–62
  Why do you need
    emotions working
    for you not against
    you?, 154–56
  Why do you need to
    find something
    that inspires you?,
    160–62
  Why do you need to
    understand and
    control worry?,
    156–57
  Why is enthusiasm
    important?, 154–55
  Why is it important
    to decide what's
    important?, 157–60
  getting ready for, 2–3
  goal lists and priority lists
    for, 140

goal setting and,
100–101
habits and, 92–93
home-work balance and,
136
Good Life Rules, 3–4, 41
choosing to be faithful.
See Faithfulness
creating new habits.
See Habits
diminishing intent.
See Diminishing
intent rule
getting to why in life: the
Eat plan. See EAT
plan; Why in life
sharing knowledge.
See Leaders
streamlining your life.
See Home-work
balance
willingness to change.
See Change
willingness to learn.
See Learning

Habits, 87–88
assessing your, 92
defining your good and
bad, 91–94
ending, 94
Good Life, The, 92
knowledge and, 89
path of least resistance
and, 89–90
physical component of, 89
for setting goals, 97–102

sources of good and bad,
88–90
starting, 94–97
Hard times, faithfulness and,
72–76
Help, asking for, change and,
17–18
Holding patterns, breaking
out of, 28–29
Holtz, Lou, 24, 97–98, 100
Home-work balance, 133–34
checking off your wins for,
142–43
dialing in your focus for,
141–42
establishing lists for,
137–39
establishing priorities for,
139–40
fallacy of scheduling for,
134–36
forty-eight-hour action
plan for, 147
perspective and, 146–47
protecting your "place" for,
143–45
steps for finding your,
136–43
Home-work lines, drawing,
19

If you can't change the
people, change the
people law of leadership,
111–13
Instincts, following your,
62–64

Integrity, 114
It never gets better than
    the interview law of
    leadership, 108–11

Kate's story, diminishing
    intent rule and
Knowing who you are,
    leadership and, 119–26

Laws of Leadership, Three
    if you can't change the
        people, change the
        people, 111–13
    it never gets better than
        the interview, 108–11
    when you're put in charge,
        take charge, 107–8
Leaders
    critical characteristics of
        great, 127–30
    effective, 108
    forty-eight-hour action
        plan for, 130–31
    knowing who you are and,
        119–29
    Talent DNA program for,
        120–26
    ways to become better, 113–19
Leadership, 105–6
    knowing who you are and,
        119–26
    ownership of, 114–19
        changing your walk/
            posture and, 116
        embracing being role
            model and, 117

finding your true talent
    and, 117–19
keeping promises and,
    115
sharing your mistakes
    and, 116–17
stop blaming and,
    115–16
Three Laws of, 106–13
    if you can't change
        the people, change
        the people,
        111–13
    it never gets better than
        the interview,
        108–11
    when you're put in
        charge, take
        charge, 107–8
Learning, 21–22
    books and, 22–25
    forty-eight-hour action
        plan for, 34–35
    for new careers,
        25–27
Letting go, 81–84
Levy, Neil, 64–65
Lists
    for change, 17
    for commitment, 84
    for faithfulness, 84
    for finding home-work
        balance, 137–39
    no, 17, 19
    priority vs. goal, 140
Looking up, change and,
    11–13

Marvel, Mark, 154
Mistakes, sharing your,
    ownership of leadership
    and, 116–17
Murdock, Mike, 15

No lists, 17
    forty-eight-hour action
        plan for, 19

Ownership of leadership. *See
    also* Leaders; Leadership
    changing your walk/
        posture and, 116
    embracing being a role
        model and, 117
    finding your true talent
        and, 117–19
    keeping promises and, 115
    sharing your mistakes and,
        116–17
    stop blaming and, 115–16

Path of least resistance, habits
    and, 89–90
Peale, Norman Vincent, 24
Perspective
    great leaders and, 129–30
    home-work balance and,
        146–47
Plans
    for change, 17
    executing, 18
Posture, ownership of
    leadership and, 116
Potential, great leaders and,
    128

*Power of Positive Thinking,
    The* (Peale), 24
Preparation, great leaders
    and, 128
Priorities
    establishing, for home-
        work balance,
        139–40
    finding your, 80–81
Priority lists, goal lists vs.,
    140
Promises, keeping, ownership
    of leadership and, 115

Questions, for The Good
    Life
    Why do you need
        emotions for you not
        against you?, 154–56
    Why do you need to
        find something that
        inspires you, 160–62
    Why do you need to
        understand and
        control worry?, 156–57
    Why is enthusiasm
        important?, 153–54
    Why is it important
        to decide what's
        important?, 157–60

Reading. *See also* Books,
    learning and
    for other people, 29–32
    steps for incorporating,
        into your life,
        32–34

Resistance, path of least, habits and, 89–90

Resolutions, forty-eight-hour, 56–58

commitment to following your heart to, 58–62

Rohn, Jim, 160

Role models, embracing being, ownership of leadership and, 117

Rudy, Matt, 144–45

Rules, for The Good Life, 3–4, 41

choosing to be faithful. *See* Faithfulness

creating new habits. *See* Habits

diminishing intent. *See* Diminishing intent rule

getting to why in life: the EAT plan. *See* EAT plan; Why in life

sharing knowledge. *See* Leaders

streamlining your life. *See* Home-work balance

willingness to change. *See* Change

willingness to learn. *See* Learning

Scheduling, Fallacy of, 134–36

Sharing knowledge rule, 3

Streamlining your life rule, 3

Surroundings, evaluating, for change, 13–16

Taking charge, 107–8

Talent, finding your true, ownership of leadership and, 117–19

Talent DNA program, 120–26

Thankfulness component, of EAT plan, 47–51

Three Laws of Leadership, 106–13

if you can't change the people, change the people, 111–13

it never gets better than the interview, 108–11

when you're put in charge, take charge, 107–8

True talent, finding your, ownership of leadership and, 117–19

Wakeup calls, for ownership of leadership, 130–31

Walk, changing your, ownership of leadership and, 116

When you're put in charge, take charge law of leadership, 107–8

Why, adding, to your vocabulary, 39–40

Why in life
   forty-eight-hour action
      plan for, 51–52
   getting to, 37–39
"Why" questions, for The
   Good Life, 153–62
   Why do you need
      emotions working for
      you not against you?,
      154–56
   Why do you need to
      find something that
      inspires you?, 160–62
   Why do you need to
      understand and
      control worry?, 156–57

Why is enthusiasm
   important?, 154–55
   Why is it important
      to decide what's
      important?, 157–58
Why Traps, avoiding, 40–42
Willingness to change rule, 3
Willingness to learn rule, 3
Wins, checking off your, for
   home-work balance,
   142–43
Work, balancing See Home-
   work balance
Worry, why you need to
   understand and control,
   156–57